THE YEAR OF THE
INTROVERT

A JOURNAL OF DAILY INSPIRATION
FOR THE INWARDLY INCLINED

MICHAELA
CHUNG

Skyhorse Publishing

Skyhorse Publishing books may be purchased in bulk at special discounts for sales promotion, corporate gifts, fund-raising, or educational purposes. Special editions can also be created to specifications. For details, contact the Special Sales Department, Skyhorse Publishing, 307 West 36th Street, 11th Floor, New York, NY 10018 or info@skyhorsepublishing.com.

Skyhorse® and Skyhorse Publishing® are registered trademarks of Skyhorse Publishing, Inc.®, a Delaware corporation.

Visit our website at www.skyhorsepublishing.com.

10 9 8 7 6 5 4 3 2 1

Library of Congress Cataloging-in-Publication Data is available on file.

Cover design by Jenny Zemanek
Cover photo credit: iStockphoto

Print ISBN: 978-1-5107-3245-2
Ebook ISBN: 978-1-5107-3246-9

Printed in China

I dedicate this book to all the introverts who have ever felt like you just don't belong and never will. I hope you feel a sense of warmth and acceptance as you make your way through these pages.

I also dedicate this book to the matriarchs of my family: my mother, Jane Darling, and my grandmother, Sylvia Adams. Your encouragement gave me courage to make my own path.

Table of Contents

Introduction

"Very little is needed to make a happy life; it is all within yourself, in your way of thinking."
—Marcus Aurelius

It is often our perception of things, rather than the things themselves, that causes us the greatest struggle. No one knows this better than introverts who spend a lot of time inside our own head. For a long time, we perceived our introversion as one of our biggest problems. We got used to people discounting our vast array of unique gifts and perspectives and reducing us to one-dimensional characters—"the quiet guy," "the serious girl," "the stoic one." The word *stoicism* itself is a great example of how perception changes everything. Once a noble school of philosophy practiced by great minds like Marcus Aurelius and Seneca, stoicism now describes someone who is "emotionless."

The meaning of the word *introversion* is constantly changing, too. For a while it seemed to be evolving in the wrong direction. In 2010, the American Psychiatric Association even considered including introversion in its Diagnostic and Statistical Manual, designating it as a contributing factor in diagnosing certain personality disorders. Thankfully they didn't go forward with the inclusion, and in the years that followed, introverts have made many strides to remove the stigma from the word.

As people are finally starting to understand that introversion is not a disorder or an affliction, we are embracing a more simplistic definition. Introverts are people who gain energy in solitude and lose energy in stimulating environments. We understand that although introverts share many little quirks and preferences, such as our hatred of phone calls and our disdain for small talk, we are each unique. Instead of feeling pressured to turn ourselves into extroverts, we have the freedom to explore what introversion means to us.

Now that we know it is possible to live life on our own terms, we wonder where to begin. We find ourselves asking the very same questions that our distant ancestors, the Ancient Stoics, once pondered:

What is the best way to live?
How can I deal with life's difficulties?
What is my obligation to my fellow human beings?
How should I handle my power?

It is the last question that I believe is especially important for introverts to consider right now. Books like Susan Cain's *Quiet*, and Laurie Helgoe's *Introvert Power* have made it clear that introverts do, indeed, have power. But many of us don't know how to tap into our power in our everyday life. It is just too abstract a concept to think that all the traits we used to be ashamed of—our quietness, slowness of speech, and love of being alone—can actually be strengths that enrich our lives.

The Year of the Introvert will help you to embrace your introverted strengths in your day-to-day life. You'll have the opportunity to do what you do best, which is to turn inward and reflect. You'll also ask yourself the important questions that lead to a happy and fulfilling life and find inspiration in daily doses of wisdom made just for you.

Although I try to address the traits and challenges many introverts share, keep in mind that introversion and extroversion occur on a spectrum. This means that there are different degrees of introversion. No one person is completely an introvert or completely an extrovert. Although we share many qualities, each introvert is unique, and thus, you might find that you don't relate to everything in this book, and that's okay. In fact, if you lean more toward the extroverted side of the spectrum, you may still see yourself in many of the entries.

We introverts are often told that we are too serious. The monthly celebrations and "fortune cookie" entries will give you the chance to approach your day with a lighthearted and hopeful mindset. Because, in the end, what keeps us getting up in the morning is hope. We are fueled by the hope that today will bring a spark of connection, a silver lining of inspiration, a sense of purpose. Above all else, our soul longs to greet each new day a little bit wiser and better than we were the day before. It is my hope that the daily entries in this book will give your soul what it desires.

Love,

Michaela

January

The Introvert Explorer

"*You enter the forest at the darkest point, where there is no path. Where there is a way or path, it is someone else's path. You are not on your own path. If you follow someone else's way, you are not going to realize your potential.*"

—Joseph Campbell, *The Hero's Journey: Joseph Campbell on His Life and Work*

January 1

THE SEASON OF BECOMING

If you've been following my work for a while, you'll know that in 2012, I quit my job, sold everything that wouldn't fit in a suitcase, and set out on my hero's journey toward a life of greater meaning and purpose. During my days as a meaning-seeking nomad, I visited twelve countries on five continents. I lived in Mexico, Australia, and Canada, and spent a good chunk of time in the US, Thailand, and Colombia.

Although I am more grounded now, my inner odyssey continues. Being the intuitive, INFP introvert that I am, I can feel when I am entering a new stage of life. I sense the winds of change before the colors fade and the leaves fall, and I just know it in my bones.

I am certain that this is a new season of life for me. The horizon is still hazy, but I know that I am smack dab in the center of what author Shauna Niequist described in her book *Bittersweet: Thoughts on Change, Grace, and Learning the Hard Way*, when she said: "There is a season for wildness and a season for settledness, and this is neither. This season is about becoming." Yes, I am becoming. Will you join me?

January 2

EMBARKING ON YOUR HERO'S JOURNEY

At the beginning of my epic odyssey toward a life of purpose, I stumbled upon Joseph Campbell's famous book, *The Hero With a Thousand Faces*, which describes The Hero's Journey, a narrative pattern found in most great movies, beloved books, and fairytales. Even religious allegories follow the story arc of The Hero's Journey.

I didn't know it at the time, but my own personal hero's journey had already begun, and it had most of the key elements of a great story:

- **A call to adventure**, which catapulted me out of the ordinary life I knew so well and onto a new and uncertain path.
- **A mentor**, who gave me advice and clues to help me on my new path.
- **Tests, allies, and enemies**. There were many naysayers who discouraged my journey.
- **The final test**, which forced me to choose between going back to my old life or defeating my greatest demons and crossing over into my new life.
- **The return home**. At the end of my journey, I came home transformed and shared the inner treasures I had discovered with other introverts.

And then I lived happily ever after. The End.

Just kidding. A true hero's journey never really ends. You'll continue to go on adventures, face trials, and find treasures. This month's entries will give you inspiration to embark on your own hero's journey.

January 3
THE CALL

Have you heard the call to adventure? At first it comes as a whisper, gently nudging you away from the life you know. It asks you to leave the dead-end relationship, the life-sucking job, the hometown you've outgrown. "Get up! Get up!" the voice says, "It's time for a new adventure." But you don't listen. You dig in your feet and make excuses. The voice gets louder and louder—so loud, in fact, that it starts shattering your excuses. The relationship breaks, the promotion falls through, and the city starts screaming at you: "You don't belong here anymore!" Now, will you listen?

January 4
JANUARY BOOK NOOK

Here is a list of books to help you with your inner explorations this month.

- *The Hero With a Thousand Faces* by Joseph Campbell
- *Wild: From Lost to Found on the Pacific Crest Trail* by Cheryl Strayed
- *Daring Greatly: How the Courage to Be Vulnerable Transforms the Way We Live, Love, Parent, and Lead* by Brené Brown
- *The Alchemist* by Paulo Coelho
- *The Four Agreements: A Practical Guide to Personal Freedom* by Don Miguel Ruiz

January 5

THE ADVENTURE

The road ahead is not straight and smooth. You'll face trials, confusion, and uncertainty. You might have a mentor to guide you, but your ultimate roadmap will arise from within. You'll have to learn to use your own inner compass to walk by starlight and trust the steps you take in the dark. You will die and be reborn again . . . and again. Hold fast to the treasures you uncover, even as your old self is perishing. One day, you will give this gold to another hero just starting out on their journey.

January 6

THE ROAD HOME

You come back to the land you once knew so well, but everything is different now. You are on the other side of your great transformation, and the world is reshaping itself around you. Share your journey's treasures with your people. You can rest for a moment, but don't fall asleep. You will need to gain strength for your next adventure.

January 7

RECOVERING WHAT WAS LOST

Have you ever caught a whiff of a familiar scent or grasped the edges of a memory that long ago escaped you? Suddenly you felt carried away by an aching to go back to that place, or person. It may surprise you to know that an unexpected call from the past is an invitation for exploration. You see, the explorer's path is not so much about charting new territory as it is about recovering what has been lost, buried, and forgotten. You can begin the excavation by looking through old photographs (Facebook makes this easy), emails, and journals.

January 8

REFLECTION QUESTIONS

What stage of The Hero's Journey do you believe you're in right now?

What aspect of yourself has been lost or forgotten on the road to adulthood?

_____

_____

_____

_____

_____

_____

January 9
Coming Home to Yourself

As an introvert explorer, your soul's goal is to come home to itself. It longs to return to that person you were years ago, when you were clumsier but also more playful; more naive but at the same time more open and optimistic. Perhaps, when you left that lover or that city or that era, you left your sense of wonder behind with it. The explorer's call is beckoning you with all its might. *Come home, come home.* It's time to retrieve what was lost.

January 10
A Friend to Walk With

"We are all just walking each other home."

—Ram Dass

Have you ever grown apart from a dear friend and, years later, wondered why? As an adolescent, I had a best friend who lived close to my house. We walked home together every day after school. Since she had been in the neighborhood longer than me, she showed me all the different paths home. I don't know how or when our friendship ended, but I do believe it served its purpose. She helped me find my way home at an age when everything felt new and confusing. From her, I learned that I do not need to walk through life alone, and neither do you.

January 11
CHOOSING A THEME FOR THE YEAR

For the last several years, I have ditched New Year's resolutions in favor of having theme years. I choose one overarching purpose for the entire year, and let it inform my decisions in the months ahead. The theme I chose last year was "Artist in Charge." I vowed to honor my inner artist throughout the year by choosing creativity over fear and letting go of "should." Try choosing a theme for this year. I recommend selecting a broad theme surrounding topics such as love, friendship, bravery, self-love, or confidence.

January 12
JANUARY FORTUNE COOKIE

Let the fortune cookie decide your fate. All you need is dice. Roll the dice, and read the fortune that coincides with the number you land on.

1. A joyful surprise awaits you.
2. A hunch is creativity trying to tell you something.
3. A good friendship is often more important than a passionate romance.
4. You'll soon make a lifelong friend.
5. A smooth, happy journey awaits you!
6. Accept what you cannot change, and life will become easier.

January 13
DECIDE YOUR TOMORROW TODAY

So much of living our most authentic life starts with the decision to do so. When I first set out to transform my blog, Introvert Spring, into an online business, I spent several hours mapping out my ideal business and lifestyle. I included how I wanted my work to make me feel, how my days would look, how many hours a day I would work, and where I would live. Today, my life and business have "magically" taken the shape I had imagined they would. The secret is that I did not simply wish my dreams into reality. I set clear intentions, and I was willing to back up my vision with action. Don't leave your future to chance. Set intentions surrounding who you want to be and how you want to live.

January 14
NAVIGATING THE CHAOS OF CHANGE

My goal used to be to lead a successful and impressive life, one that followed straight lines toward logical conclusions. Now, I am more interested in a beautiful life. I want the difficult conversations and the fork-in-the-road moments because I know that they will open my heart to love. I want the charm of simplicity—the sleep-ins, the afternoon walks, the good books. But I also want the chaos of change and the uncertainty of transformation. I know that moving onto a new stage in life is much like moving house. For a while there is a mess of clutter and confusion as you rearrange your life. But eventually, you settle into a new way of being in the world. You realize that you are finding your way home, one messy step at a time.

January 15
THE ART OF SELF-EXPLORATION

Self-exploration is an individual endeavor. Just as there is no single path to finding one's Self, there is no set way to examine her. You can get right up in her face and shake out her secrets, interrogation style. Or you can sit beside her, ask her a thoughtful question or two, and patiently wait for her response. Regardless of how you approach her, the important thing is to let yourself know that you are here to stay. You will not abandon her. You will look her in the face and be there for her every step of the way.

January 16
REFLECTION QUESTIONS

List the people who have helped "walk you home" at each stage of your life.

Is there an aspect of your life that seems out of alignment with your authentic self? This could be a relationship that doesn't quite fit, a career that doesn't match your personality, or hobbies that don't suit your needs.

_____

_____

_____

_____

January 17

Unfair Comparisons

When we see photoshopped pictures of smiling people whom we admire, it's easy to believe that their journey was smooth and straight. We assume that they never had to endure the self-doubt and failure that we face on our path. Believe me, they have had their share of struggles, too. Their lives got messy and the road ahead was uncertain, but they decided to carry on anyway. I hope that you will do the same.

January 18

Dealing with Self-Doubt

When self-doubt arises, as it does on every hero's journey, take a step back and observe your worries and self-criticisms as you would a litter of puppies playing together. There might be hungry, pathetic, hilarious, or ridiculous thoughts slobbering all over your sense of reason. But they sure are entertaining.

January 19

Transforming Your Fear

Fear is an expected companion on the explorer's path. But your fears are not as scary and insurmountable as they seem. Like an unruly child, fear simply wants your attention. If you don't look fear in the face, it will keep poking at you until you feel utterly defeated. The secret to transforming your fear into courage is to parent it. Approach it as you would a child who is suffering. Sit with it, look at it with compassion. Accept it as part of your family, part of you.

January 20
MONTHLY GRATITUDE MOMENT

"Feeling gratitude and not expressing it is like wrapping a present and not giving it."

—William Arthur Ward

What are you most thankful for this month? Make a great, big abundant list, or write in-depth about one or two things for which you are most grateful.

January 21
QUIET COURAGE

A lot of people think I'm brave because I quit my job and traveled the world alone in search of purpose. And yes, doing this required a lot of courage. But for introverts like me, there are things that scare us even more than performing or traveling solo. At the top of the list might be saying "I love you" for the first time, or opening up to someone new. Remember, the bravest acts happen in quiet moments. When you feel afraid to speak up or try something new, but you do it anyway, you are the definition of courage.

January 22
Be Forgetful

The best way to reclaim your life and make it truly your own is to forget. Forget the way you should behave. Forget the shame you've been carrying as if it were a hidden weapon against yourself. Forget the person you were trying to be to please others. Forget all the answers you blindly accepted, and start asking questions. Question your beliefs about yourself—your limitations as well as your expectations for your future. Question your faith, or lack thereof. Question your grand plans and your narrow view. The time for sleeping has passed.

January 23
It's Never Too Late

Our inner explorations, have a way of rejuvenating us. Somehow, opening the door to old memories allows in a gust of new possibilities. Best all, our inner treasures don't have an expiry date. They return to their original luster the moment we uncover and reclaim them. I once read about a type of ferry shrimp that lives in potholes in West Africa. These tiny shrimp can lose as much as 92 percent of their body moisture—basically becoming microscopic shrimp chips—and plump right back up the moment water returns. Self-exploration is like this. Looking inward with compassion and curiosity helps us to feel whole and new again.

January 24

Reflection Questions

What will your theme be for this year? It helps to first review your core values and deepest desires and let them inform your overarching purpose for the year.

What would your perfect day look like? Describe the day from morning to night and include details, such as where you live, how and with whom you spend your morning, and how you feel.

_____

_____

_____

January 25

Curing the Urge to Escape

I'm restless. Things are calling me away. My hair is being pulled by the stars again."
— Anaïs Nin, _Fire: From A Journal of Love_

After my epic Hero's Journey across continents, I became accustomed to an untethered life. I was always setting my sights toward the horizon for fulfillment. I never imagined that I would create the freedom-based "laptop lifestyle," which I still enjoy today. Nowadays, I feel no need to escape my life. I can go anywhere at any time, but I mostly don't. My goal is to make my everyday reality so good that I don't need to run away from it. You can do the same by asking yourself, *What would make my everyday reality so sweet that I don't want to escape it?*

January 26
The Selfish Path to Purpose

My personal journey toward a life of meaning and purpose has been undeniably selfish. And yet, I see now that even as I lived so selfishly, I was able to help others in ways I never imagined. My selfish path has allowed me to touch millions of lives. What difference would I have made in the world if I had "unselfishly" stayed in a job I hated and lived my life according to other people's expectations? I can't imagine that I would have made much of an impact; plus I would have been miserable. If you feel like it's selfish to follow your own path, try to see the bigger picture and imagine how much more your authentic self can offer to the world.

January 27
Prioritizing Purpose

Whenever I do consultation calls with potential coaching clients, I always ask them to tell me their top three goals for the year. Oftentimes, their goals align with the challenge for which they are seeking coaching. For example, if they want introvert dating coaching, finding a partner is one of their top three goals. There have been many times, however, when there is a glaring discrepancy between the person's goals and the challenge for which they are seeking coaching. This tells me that they probably aren't truly ready to change their circumstances. If you really want to find your purpose this year, make it a priority. Add it to the top of your list of goals, and let it influence all your decisions.

January 28
EXPLORER'S CHALLENGE

Chip away at one of your secret fears this month. Don't worry, you don't need to conquer your fear all at once. Take a more gradual approach by exposing yourself to your fear one small step at a time. For example, if you are afraid of speaking in public, write a one-hundred-word speech and read it in front of a close friend or two. If you are afraid of flirting with your love interests, try simply making eye contact for one second with an attractive stranger.

January 29
RELAXING INTO CHANGE

I used to have a recurring dream that my tooth was loose and about to fall out. In every dream, I would panic and try to force the tooth back in again. If you're into dream interpretation, you might already know that loose tooth dreams represent life change or transition. You also know that change is scary. Just like I did in my dream, you might be tempted to do whatever you can to keep things the same. But change is necessary, and also inevitable. Help it along by relaxing into it instead of trying to force your way back into your old life.

January 30
KNOWING YOUR CORE VALUES

A major aspect of living an authentic life is honoring your values. In order to do this, you must know what is most important to you. Make a list of at least ten of your values. Your list might include things like creativity, authenticity, integrity, honesty, passion, excellence, spirituality, and connection.

Next, circle the top five values that matter most to you. Now that you know your core values, write them on cue cards and place them where you will see them every day. You can also rewrite them in your journal each day, so they are always at the forefront of your heart and mind.

January 31
JANUARY CELEBRATION

A core teaching, which I weave into all of my introvert courses and coaching programs, is to celebrate your success, no matter how small. Some things that you might celebrate include:

- Trying out one of the tools you learned in this book
- Starting a new project
- Standing up for yourself
- Adopting a new healthy habit
- Making progress on an important project
- Opening up to someone new

You don't have to wait until you've achieved your biggest goals to give yourself a pat on the back. Write down this month's celebration in your journal.

February

SELF-LOVE SECRETS

"Confront the dark parts of yourself, and work to banish them with illumination and forgiveness. Your willingness to wrestle with your demons will cause your angels to sing."
—August Wilson

February 1
Broken to Open

In mid-January 2014, I arrived at the Mexico City airport in the middle of the night. After spending a tumultuous year in Latin America in search of purpose and meaning (which I found in spades, by the way), I was heading back to Canada. My epic journey was over . . . or so I thought.

It had been a rough year. Even though I'd found my life's purpose by creating my blog *Introvert Spring*, I'd also experienced what it was like to be beyond broke, alone, and heartbroken. Would the near future be any brighter? I honestly didn't know.

I spent several hours sitting in silence in the eerily empty airport. As more and more people sleep-walked into the waiting room, I turned on my beat-up Blackberry Tablet and read *A Return to Love* by Marianne Williamson. I had been reading the book for a while, but at that moment, her words came alive. They wrapped around me like a loving embrace and inspired me to do something I'd never done before.

I pulled out my journal and wrote a love letter to myself. It began, "I love this woman because," and went on to outline in sincere detail all the reasons why I was proud, grateful, and happy to be exactly the woman I am.

Tears streamed down my face, as my own words now held me in a warm embrace. People were starting to look at me with concern, but I didn't care. I knew something big had just happened.

In that moment at the airport, I fell deeply and unconditionally in love with the person with whom I'm meant to spend the rest of my life: me.

In the weeks that followed, I experienced all the typical symptoms of being in love. All my senses seemed to be heightened. Everything around me was brighter and more beautiful, and I felt more confident and joyous than I had ever felt before. Because I was so brimming with love, I couldn't help but be kind to those around me, but it was also more than that.

I was really and truly kind to myself. It was as if the love letter I'd written had become part of me. I continuously chanted uplifting words to myself. Of course, that self-love high didn't last forever. As the months wore on, there were times when life got less shiny. Still, the self-love seed had been firmly planted. This month, I'll share some secrets to help you turn the page on your own self-love story and fall in love with you.

February 2
More Love to Go Around

After falling in love with myself, I discovered that self-love makes loving others feel natural. This was a real revelation to me, as I am by nature a very self-protective person. Like a lot of introverts, my default coping mechanism for stress is to push people away rather than let them in. But every time I experience a surge in self-love, I suddenly feel more comfortable giving and receiving love from others. As you go through your day today, make a point to love yourself first, knowing that doing so will make it easier for you to love others.

February 3
Mental Clarity

Do you have a tendency to overthink and self-criticize? Self-love brings mental clarity. It boots out the bad guys in your brain, leaving more room for constructive ideas and decisions. Imagine how freeing it would be to get rid of the nasty, critical voices in your mind. You can start your journey toward smart self-love the same way I did, by writing a love letter to yourself. Write it in the third person, and don't be modest!

February 4
February Book Nook

Here are some books to help you cultivate self-love.

1. *A Return to Love: Reflections on the Principles of "A Course in Miracles"* by Marianne Williamson
2. *You Are a Badass: How to Stop Doubting Your Greatness and Start Living an Awesome Life* by Jen Sincero
3. *Shadows Before Dawn: Finding the Light of Self-Love Through Your Darkest Times* by Teal Swan
4. *The Gifts of Imperfection: Let Go of Who You Think You're Supposed to Be and Embrace Who You Are* by Brené Brown
5. *Love Yourself Like Your Life Depends On It* by Kamal Ravikant

February 5
A New Destiny

If you've repeatedly experienced heartbreak, rejection, and failure, you might be tempted to think that you're just destined to feel lonely and unhappy. Self-love alters that destiny. Falling in love with myself in the airport in Mexico paved the way toward more love in the future. It allowed me to let in love in all its forms. It's impossible to know how self-love might change your destiny. But I'm pretty sure it will bring more love of all sorts into your life. Plus a little bit of magic.

February 6
Forgetting How To Love

"I think the reward for conformity is that everyone likes you except yourself."
—Rita Mae Brown

When we lower our standards, live a lie, wear a mask, and forget who we are, we also forget how to love ourselves. After all, it's hard to love someone we don't even know. Choose to show yourself love today by remembering who you are, where you came from, what you stand for, and what you have to offer the world. Remember how far you've come and how much you've overcome to get here.

February 7
Loving Yourself First

The other day, I watched a TEDX talk by a woman named Lilia Tarawa entitled "I grew up in a cult. It was heaven—and hell." Tarawa did not muster the courage to leave the cult until she saw her family and friends being abused and humiliated. It wasn't enough for just *her* to suffer abuse. This made her wonder why she didn't love herself enough to protect herself. Although most people do not know what it's like to grow up in a cult, many can relate to Tarawa's lack of self-love. Hopefully, you'll never have to endure such a traumatic experience to make loving and protecting yourself a priority.

February 8
Reflection Questions

Have you ever stood up for someone you loved but failed to do the same for yourself? If so, why was it so hard to love yourself as much as you loved your friend or family member?

Make a list of self-love activities you will do this week.

_____

_____

_____

_____

_____

February 9

LOVING YOURSELF WHEN YOU'VE MESSED UP

It's hard to be self-loving when you feel like you've messed up. Perhaps you're like me, and you grew up thinking that you had to earn love, even from yourself. When you feel like you've done something wrong, your first instinct might be to scold yourself. So instead of getting critical when you make a mistake, get curious by asking "what":

- What is the lesson here?
- What was my deeper motivation for doing that?
- What could I do differently next time?

February 10

LET YOUR ACTIONS DO THE LOVING

Do you know the old saying, "Actions speak louder than words"? This is particularly true when it comes to loving ourselves. When we do kind things for ourselves, we feel important and loved. Just like in any relationship with a partner, your love affair with you doesn't need to be grandiose. It's the small, consistent gestures that have the biggest impact over time. Here are some ideas:

- Buy a little treat that you normally wouldn't splurge on, such as a scented candle, specialty coffee, or pretty nail polish.
- Light some candles and take a luxurious bubble bath.
- Take a break. And breathe.
- Surprise your future self by hiding five-dollar bills in coat sleeves or party purses.

February 11
Love Yourself by Accepting Support

Another essential self-care practice is accepting support from others. For most introverts, our natural reaction to stress is to close off and turn inward. That's not entirely a bad thing, except that self-critical thoughts tend to grow wild in isolation. Just saying your problems out loud and feeling heard can lessen the weight of your worries. Accept support today by being candid with a close friend about your fears and issues.

February 12
February Fortune Cookie

Let the fortune cookie decide your fate. Roll the dice, and read the fortune that coincides with the number you land on.

1. Adventure can be true happiness.
2. Your troubles will soon pass, and you'll reach calm waters.
3. A special person will offer you support.
4. Someone from your past will greet you in the near future.
5. All your hard work will be handsomely rewarded soon.
6. A touch of love will bring out your inner poet.

February 13
Give in to Your Own Conditions

If you're like a lot of introverts I know, your subconscious harbors deeply ingrained stipulations about what makes you worthy of love. For example, you might believe that you are only loveable if you are a good person, and that you are only a good person if you respect your parents, help the needy, and achieve your goals. When it comes to cultivating self-love, it's essential that you set aside most of these conditions and simply love yourself, even when you don't feel like you've earned it. But of course it also helps to do the things that will make you feel worthy. For example, by giving to those less fortunate than you, you will feel that it's alright to give to yourself. Submit to your own conditions if you must, but remember that you deserve love, even when you fall short of them.

February 14
Fill Your Own Cup

Have you ever looked to another person to rescue you from yourself? You wanted them to fill the void that aches inside you and validate your very existence. In other words, you wanted them to do your job. Filling your own cup may be tiring, frustrating work, but it is your lifelong duty, nonetheless. Though you may not always see it, you are paid handsomely for your efforts. When you fill your own cup, you will have more energy, love, and patience to go around. If you have been feeling neglected by a friend, lover, or family member, ask yourself how you can fill the spaces they have failed to fill.

February 15
Self-Love vs. Selfishness

Is self-love selfish? Many people believe it is. It's true that self-love and selfishness do share some similarities—selfishness means that you put your own needs above the needs of others; likewise, self-love requires that you prioritize your own needs. However, it's not always black and white. Self-love is going left when those who love you tell you to go right—not because you want to hurt them but rather because you no longer want to hurt yourself. Having self-love is daring to imagine a life for yourself that is more full, luscious, and alive than what others have in mind for you.

February 16
Reflection Questions

Think back to a time when you felt the most in love with yourself. Who were your friends, what were your hobbies, where were you living? Can you replicate this?

What are some of your "conditions" for self-love? In other words, what do you feel you have to do in order to be worthy of love?

_____

_____

_____

_____

February 17
Duty Is Not the Same as Love

There is a big difference between duty and love. Yet, many of us live a life driven by obligation, and we try to call it love. The same goes for self-love—we fulfill the bare minimum of required duties to ourselves. We feed and support ourselves, put a roof over our own head, and believe that this should be enough. But it isn't. Just as a mother shows her child love through affection, protection, and devotion, we, too, must learn to love ourselves in invisible ways—not out of duty, but out of genuine compassion and care.

February 18
Be More Disappointing

I have a confession. I am not a people-pleaser. In fact, I'm pretty much the opposite of a people-pleaser—what is that? I suppose I'm a people-disappointer. I'm sorry to be so disappointing, but at the same time, I've learned to accept that I just don't have the energy to make everyone happy. I share this in the hopes that if you are a people-pleaser, you will realize that it's okay to disappoint others. It's not your job to be an endless source of pleasure for those you care about—that's what the Internet is for. Also, you don't need to earn love with constant giving. You're worthy of love just as you are.

February 19
Love Yourself Today by Letting Go

Let go of the need to fix the past and predict the future. Both are impossible.

Let go of the urge to know the next steps, to have it all figured out, to be perfect.

Let go of the should-haves, and the might-have-beens.

Let go of the need to control.

See how it feels to unclench your fists, and let your hands be hands instead of weapons against yourself.

Let go of the need to know if you're doing something right or if you should have done more.

More is not your mecca.

You are enough just as you are.

February 20
Monthly Gratitude Moment

Why are you grateful to be exactly the person you are today? Make a list of the qualities you are thankful for. Or, focus in on one or two key qualities and write about them to your heart's content.

February 21
Love Yourself Today by Just Being

Be wrong, be right, be strong, be weak, be fierce, be afraid—be whatever your heart wants you to be in this moment. First and foremost, be honest. The worst thing to be is a lie.

February 22

Love Yourself Today by Relaxing

Relax the muscles in your body; they have been tensed for too long.

Set down the weight of your own expectations.

You don't need to get an A+ at life.

Soften into your imperfections, knowing that humanness is an incurable condition.

Acceptance is the only answer to not having all the answers.

February 23

Love Yourself Today by Forgiving

Forgive yourself for making mistakes, realizing too late, and not reading the fine print.

Analyzing is not the same as accepting.

Forgive yourself for going into debt, forgetting to return the phone call, leaving words unsaid.

Holding on is not the same as healing.

Forgive yourself for laughing at the wrong time and crying over the wrong person.

Regretting is not the same as fixing.

Forgive yourself for being too much for some and not enough for others.

Measuring is not the same as moving on.

February 24

Reflection Questions

What or who do you need to let go of in order to love yourself more freely?

What do you need to forgive yourself for in order to be more self-loving? Write a forgiveness letter to yourself.

_____

_____

_____

_____

_____

_____

February 25

Love Yourself Today by Becoming

Become the kind of person who knows how to laugh from the bottom of their belly and love from the center of their soul.

Become less of someone else and more of yourself; less of an apology and more of a declaration.

Become that person you can just barely see when you squint your eyes and imagine someone who is worthy.

Set down the pretending, the hoping, the dreaming. This is the era of becoming.

February 26
The L.O.V.E Method for Self-Love

When introverts are feeling drained and overwhelmed, the little troll in our brain comes out to play. He tells us that we are unworthy of love; heck, according to the troll, we are not even likeable. All of our worst insecurities rise to the surface, and we feel worthless. My L.O.V.E Method will help you stop the troll in his tracks and get yourself back to a more self-loving state.

Lean back
Take a moment to gain some mental and/or physical distance from the situation. Imagine that you're looking at what is happening from a safe vantage point several yards away.

Observe
The next step is simply to observe what is occurring without judgment. Also observe how you're feeling. Put a label on the emotion. For example, you might say, "Oh, that nausea in my stomach is fear," or "This tense feeling is me feeling overwhelmed."

Vote for you
When your favorite team starts losing, do you immediately start cheering for the other team? Probably not. And yet, most of us spend our whole lives voting for the other guy.
To develop a self-loving mindset, you must consistently be on your own side. This means having compassion for yourself when you feel like you're losing at the game of life.

Escape
The troll brain is usually cruelest when you are tired and overwhelmed. The best way to silence it is to seek out space and solitude. If you are already by yourself, escaping might mean going outside or distracting yourself with one of your favorite hobbies.

February 27
Self-Love Challenge

In Teal Swan's book *Shadows Before Dawn* she recommends that anytime you are faced with a decision, great or small, you should ask yourself, "What would someone who loves themselves do?" Swan challenges readers to ask themselves this question for an entire year. That is a great goal, but for now, let's start with one day. Anytime you have to make a decision for the next twenty-four hours, ask yourself what someone who loves themselves would do.

February 28
Call on an Intermediary

Sometimes, the thought of loving ourselves is too abstract. We need an intermediary, someone to translate our feeble expressions of affection into pure, unconditional love. For many, God is that intermediary. We can only feel self-love when we see ourselves through the eyes of the great Creator. A spiritual life in general—or even a creative life, which I hold equal to a spiritual life—serves as a shortcut to self-love. If you can't love yourself just as you are, love your God, Source, the Universe, or an enlightened guru, and let Him/Her/It/All reflect that love back to you.

February 29
February Celebration

That which you focus on grows, so it's important to bring your attention to the positives. Write down something you would like to celebrate today—it might be an accomplishment or experience—and take action. It could be as simple as making a phone call you've been putting off or getting out for a daily walk.

March

Creative Awakening

"Adults follow paths. Children explore. Adults are content to walk the same way, hundreds of times, or thousands; perhaps it never occurs to adults to step off the paths, to creep beneath rhododendrons, to find the spaces between fences."
　　　　—Neil Gaiman, *The Ocean at the End of the Lane*

WHY CREATIVITY?

Even though many introverts are highly creative, we might not see the value in this gift. We wonder, why even bother with something as frivolous as creativity when there are bills to pay, disasters to mourn, and children to raise? Isn't creativity a luxury for the young and impractical? What's the point?

Well. If you're a creative introvert like me, the call to create is strong—so strong, in fact, that if you ignore it there are unexpected consequences. I think Elizabeth Gilbert sums it up perfectly in her book *Big Magic: Creative Living Beyond Fear* when she says, "If I am not actively creating something, then I am probably actively destroying something—myself, a relationship, or my own peace of mind."

Do you feel that burning urge to build, construct, and create? And have you noticed that when you ignore it, you become anxious and restless? Perhaps that's when you start hunting for imperfections, like me—you find flaws in your life and in yourself. You create and amplify problems.

After all, creative energy is life force energy. Accessing and unleashing your creativity impacts every area of your life. It paints over the dull parts and brings some color back into your existence. It revives your curiosity and makes life interesting again.

March 2

You Have Something to Share

You've got something up your sleeve, I just know it. It's a book, a script, a painting, a photograph, a dream. This thing you've kept hidden away like a dirty secret is itching to get out. It's creating scratch marks on your insides. It wants to be born. Will you let it?

March 3

Speaking the Language of Creativity

The creative voice, which I call the Inner Artist, has her own unique way of communicating. Much of the time, your Artist is banging her head against the walls of your ego, wondering why you can't understand her messages. From her perspective, speaking to you is like having a conversation with a chatty extrovert who only wants to hear the sound of his own voice.

Luckily, the solution is simple. It's the same antidote you would use to repair a real-life relationship: listen. Stop speaking over your Artist and trying to bully her into conversation. Simply sit patiently with her and allow her to speak up when and how she pleases.

March 4

March Book Nook

Here are my top book recommendations to reawaken your Inner Artist.

- *Big Magic: Creative Living Beyond Fear* by Elizabeth Gilbert
- *On Writing: A Memoir of The Craft* by Stephen King
- *The Artist's Way* by Julia Cameron
- *Bird by Bird: Some Instructions on Writing and Life* by Anne Lamott
- *Steal Like an Artist* by Austin Kleon

March 5

The Artist vs. The Manager

Your Inner Artist isn't the only one influencing your creativity, or lack thereof. You also have an Inner Manager, otherwise known as your logical self. His primary role is to keep the Artist safe so she doesn't go broke or set herself on fire as she pursues her dreams. You see, both roles are important. But most of us have forgotten who the real star of the show is. We think the Manager is the headliner; in truth, the Artist is meant to take center stage. Let's put her back where she belongs, shall we?

March 6

PUT THE MANAGER IN HIS PLACE

The manager has his place, but it is not the stage or the blank page. Let me put it this way, the manager helps you get to the performance, but he doesn't come on stage with you. Also, don't glorify the Manager. He's an alright guy, but he takes himself way too seriously. Meanwhile, your Artist is a creative badass. She knows your soul's secrets, including how to unlock your true artistic potential.

March 7

WOOING THE ARTIST

Creativity is a lot like an introvert: if you put her on the spot, she shuts down or hides. But if you sit with her patiently and consistently, she shares wonderful and surprising secrets. Give your Inner Artist room to come out of her shell in her own due time. Let her know that you'll be there when she's ready to open up by showing up for her each day.

March 8

Reflection Questions

What would you create if it didn't have to be logical or practical?

What can you do this week to woo your Artist? Your list might include daily rituals, spending time in nature, or a promise to simply show up and listen.

March 9

Choose Curiosity Over Fear

Fear is inevitable when you are making art, but curiosity can soften its sharp edges. Curiosity says, "I don't have all the answers, but I'm open to learning." Meanwhile, fear is only interested in what is known and certain. Get curious about the people you encounter in your daily life. Better still, get curious about your own beliefs, desires, and fears. Where did they come from, and where might they take you?

March 10

Put the Gun Down

Many of us pressure our Inner Artist to produce her best work on the spot. We put a gun to her head, and say, "Gimme all your creativity, or I'll shoot." She doesn't respond very well to this approach. What works better is to be like the old man I used to see floating by my window in his little red and white sailboat. This man would spend hours drifting along, enjoying the scenery, as he set his sails toward no destination in particular. Your Artist prefers to feel like you are on a pleasure sail together, enjoying the journey, instead of rushing toward a set destination.

March 11

Don't Put Your Artist in a Box

Many of us try to cordon off our creativity, restricting her to one dingy corner of our life. We tell our Artist that we can only see her on Saturday mornings before eleven. But creativity can't be put in a neat little box. She wants to spill over the edges and tap you on the shoulder at inconvenient times. Thankfully, your Artist is one of the most delightful uninvited guests an introvert could hope for. Give her the keys to your apartment, your office, or your garden shed, and allow her to come and go as she pleases. Keep a small notebook in your pocket so that you are always ready for her arrival.

March 12

MARCH FORTUNE COOKIE

Let the fortune cookie decide your fate. Roll the dice, and read the fortune that coincides with the number you land on.

1. The sloth is patient, the rabbit disingenuous.
2. The time to act is now! Delay no more!
3. Staying close to home will boost your morale today.
4. An old friend will reach out to you soon.
5. Stand tall. Don't look down on yourself.
6. You will look to your family for comfort this month.

March 13

GIVE HER COMMITMENT AND ROMANCE

Creativity is not a cheap date that you can ignore most of the week and then give a booty call whenever you please. She requires commitment and romance. Set aside time to create each day. Julia Cameron, author of *The Artist's Way*, also recommends taking yourself on an "Artist Date" once a week. An Artist Date involves making time for yourself to do something enchanting. It doesn't have to be extravagant or expensive—you could visit a local museum, go for a walk in the forest, watch a foreign movie, or listen to live music. Your Artist Dates will keep your creativity turned on.

SMALL CHANGES THAT AWAKEN THE ARTIST

If you've been letting your Inner Manager take center stage for too long, you likely feel blocked. Luckily, you don't need to do anything extreme to get out of your rut. Simply wake up at a different time. Or go for a walk at dawn. Take a bath instead of a shower. Go left instead of right. Say yes, instead of no. Small changes to your daily routine will get you off autopilot and into the present moment. This is key because your Inner Artist can only get through to you when you're paying attention.

March 15

REDISCOVERING YOUR EMOTIONS

Your Artist's favorite way to communicate with you is through your emotions. Unfortunately, we live in a culture that encourages us to disconnect from and suppress our feelings. To awaken your intuition and reconnect with your Inner Artist, you must begin actually feeling and identifying your emotions on a daily—ideally minute-by-minute—basis.

Begin by doing emotion check-ins throughout your day, and try to pinpoint what you are feeling at a given moment. You can even set a reminder on your phone to go off two to three times per day.

March 16

REFLECTION QUESTIONS

How can you change your routine this week and get out of autopilot?

What emotions did you feel throughout your day today?

What emotion are you feeling right now?

_____

_____

_____

_____

_____

_____

March 17

THE HELLO GAME

An easy way to start noticing the world around you is to play what I call "The Hello Game."

Don't worry, the Hello Game has nothing to do with greeting passersby. It is all about acknowledging what you see in front of you. Lift your head from your noisy thoughts and take a moment to greet a lovely lilac tree, or a squirrel, or the sun. A simple "Hello tree, I appreciate you" will do wonders. This easy practice will awaken you to the world of inspiration that is unfolding right in front of your eyes.

March 18

FOCUSING ON YOUR SENSES

One of the best ways to reconnect with your creativity is to get into your body. You can do this by honing in on your senses: touch, smell, taste, sight, sound. Reconnect with your body today by spending a few moments focusing all your attention on one sense. If you choose sight, avoid the urge to just look *at* things. Instead, look *into* them. Look straight into the sunset sky and allow the colors to fill your eyes.

March 19

GETTING CURIOUS

They say curiosity killed the cat, but that was only the tenth time. During his other nine lives, the cat relished in the boons of his curiosity. He loved how it made his day more interesting and alive.

As you observe the world around you, get curious about what lies beyond the surface. For example, if you see a plane passing overhead, wonder who is on that plane and where they are going. Curiosity might eventually kill the cat, but it has the opposite effect on your mind. It ignites your creativity, and makes you feel alive.

March 20

Monthly Gratitude Moment

Why are you grateful to your Inner Artist? Make a long and abundant list of all the ways she has enriched your life. Or focus on one or two points, and write in-depth about why you're thankful for her influence.

March 21

Opening the Creative Channels

Many of us foolishly believe that we own our creativity. We imagine that our mind is the genius wizard working his creative magic behind the curtain. In fact, we are more like channels plugged into a greater consciousness. Our Inner Artist is the interpreter. This is a good thing because it means that we have access to information that our logical brain cannot reach on its own. What a relief it is to know that our primary responsibility is not to cultivate genius, but simply to open up the channel and listen closely.

Expecting Imperfection

"Almost all good writing begins with terrible first efforts. You need to start somewhere. Start by getting something— anything—down on paper. What I've learned to do when I sit down to work on a shitty first draft is to quiet the voices in my head."

—Anne Lamott, *Bird by Bird: Some Instructions on Writing and Life*

Come to your art with a playful and open heart. This is creativity after all! It's not life or death, but a source of aliveness. Take a deep breath, relax into the moment, and give yourself permission to produce what Anne Lamott refers to as the "shitty first draft."

Embracing the Detours

Artists don't make mistakes. We make detours, which often lead to far more fascinating destinations than what we had originally planned. Unclench your fists and come to your art with a sense of openness. Be willing to take paths you hadn't considered, even if you don't know where they may lead.

March 24

Reflection Questions

Open up a dialogue with your Inner Artist and ask her the questions below. She might not answer you right away, but simply asking the questions will allow the answers to come later in unexpected ways.

- What message would you like to share most with me right now?
- What can I do or stop doing to make it safe for you to come out and play more often?

_____

_____

_____

_____

March 25

Creating Empty Spaces

In our culture, we are told that productivity is the key to success. We don't see the value in empty spaces. But being "unproductive" is a necessary occupation of the artist. We need be able to do nothing for a while. As our mind rests, our subconscious can make connections and form ideas. Go for a leisurely walk; sit in a cafe and stare into space; or take a long train ride and spend the time listening to music, gazing out the window, and daydreaming.

March 26

Breaking the Creme Brûlée

Many of us are familiar with the saying "break the ice," but when it comes to creativity, I prefer a different term. You see, when you crack through a layer of ice, all you get is cold water. But a few gentle taps on creme brûlée and you reach a delicious treat. We break the creativity creme brûlée when we sit down at our desk each morning and set to work on a project. Even if we don't get very far, we have created an opening through which delicious ideas can flow for the rest of the day. Similarly, visiting a creative project before bed opens subconscious channels and allows answers to seep in through our dreams.

March 27

Try a New Art Form

Awaken your Artist by trying out a new form of creative expression. For example, if your art of choice is normally writing, you could try drawing. If you're a visual artist, try gardening or decorating. If you're a dancer, try poetry. It's up to you! Just keep in mind that it doesn't have to be logical or practical.

March 28

CREATIVE CHALLENGE

Create a daily creative practice and commit to it for seven days straight. Your creative practice doesn't have to be long and complicated. Even setting aside fifteen minutes in the morning to draw or write will do the trick. The point is to show up for your Artist each day, no matter how you are feeling or what else is happening in your life.

March 29

TAKE THE SIMPLE ROUTE

Life can be simple, and so can the art it inspires. And yet, as humans we feel the need to complicate, to take a long winding route to a straightforward destination. Sometimes, the simplest answer is the best answer. You write the sentence exactly how you would say it. Or you paint the picture in broad strokes instead of fussing over every minute detail. Perhaps, you'll revisit and refine later. For now, take the easy route, and just get it done.

March 30

ACKNOWLEDGE THE ARTIST'S MESSAGES

As your creative channels open, synchronicities often follow. Don't pass these occurrences off to chance. Make note of them in your journal. Write about the idea that came to you in a dream or the strange coincidences that are happening more and more. Perhaps you were thinking of exploring spoken word poetry, and a stranger told you about a slam he went to recently (this happened to me). Or the very second you thought about taking up singing again, your friend called to invite you to join her choir. Acknowledge each and every magical coincidence.

March 31

MARCH CELEBRATION

What is your celebration for this month? Remember, your celebration can be something as small and simple as expressing a difficult emotion or showing up for your Artist when you felt like quitting. Write down your celebration in your journal, and, if you feel inclined, share it with a friend or family member.

April

Energy Restoration

*"You will burn and you will burn out; you will be healed
and come back again."*
        —Fyodor Dostoyevsky, *The Brothers Karamazov*

April 1

INVISIBLE INTROVERT ENERGY

The word "energy" comes up a lot when discussing introversion. A while ago, while doing a radio show interview, the host asked me the difference between an introvert and an extrovert. I rattled off my standard answer: an introvert gains energy from being alone and loses energy in stimulating environments. He asked, "What do you mean by 'energy'; is this some sort of esoteric thing?"

I found it difficult to articulate exactly what the word *energy* means for an introvert, except to say that it is in short supply. It is an intangible resource that we can't seem to keep on the shelves. It's always getting used up, but where is it going? Extroverts direct their energy outward, where everyone can see it. Introverts, on the other hand, direct much of our energy inward, where it remains unseen.

Even though we can't see energy, we know what it looks like when it is lacking. Low energy looks like exhaustion, zoning out, irritability, and withdrawing. It's no wonder that people often think introverts are depressed. What appears to be sadness is actually our body and mind shutting down. We know that if we continue directing our energy outward by socializing, we will lose what little energy we have left. And so, we shut down, turn inward, and withdraw.

Luckily there are ways to cope with your inconsistent energy levels as an introvert. This month's insights and tools will help you to do just that.

April 2

INTROVERT ENERGY-SAVING MODE

Has anyone ever told you you're lazy? By definition, laziness is an unwillingness to use energy. As introverts, we must be lazy sometimes because our energy is limited. Sure, we can force ourselves to get out there and do as the extroverts do for a day or two. But eventually our tanks are depleted. Doing nothing helps restore us. So, I prefer not to label introverts as lazy. We're just in energy-saving mode.

April 3

YES, YOU'RE OKAY

As much as we introverts try to go under the radar, our inconsistent energy levels often attract unwanted speculation. Extroverts who meet us in social situations where our energy levels are high and we are "on" are downright stumped by our behavior when we are "introverting." Their confusion leads them to ask annoying questions like, "Why are you so quiet?" and "Are you okay?" As horrible as this might feel, know that you haven't done anything wrong. An extrovert's seemingly endless energy stores do not make them superior. You simply have different needs. Cut yourself some slack, dearest.

April 4
APRIL BOOK NOOK

Here is a list of books to help you restore your energy and refresh your life.

1. *Self-Care for the Self-Aware: A Guide for Highly Sensitive People, Empaths, Intuitives, and Healers* by David Markowitz
2. *Women's Bodies, Women's Wisdom (Revised Edition): Creating Physical and Emotional Health and Healing* by Christiane Northrup, MD
3. *The Highly Sensitive Person: How to Thrive When the World Overwhelms You* by Elaine N. Aron, PhD
4. *Emotional Freedom: Liberate Yourself from Negative Emotions and Transform Your Life* by Judith Orloff
5. *How Not to Die: Discover the Foods Scientifically Proven to Prevent and Reverse Disease* by Michael Greger, MD

April 5
When Sickness Feels Like a Relief

I don't get sick often, but when I do, I experience an unexpected sense of relief. Perhaps, you can relate to the way a rundown body allows you to slow down. You relish the opportunity to shuffle around the house, looking disheveled, as dishes pile in the sink. For once, you feel entitled to be anything but perfect. The dishes can wait, and so can everything else on your to-do list. What if you could give yourself permission to take a time-out without getting sick? What if your only occupation for the next twenty-four hours was to heal from the sheer effort of existing?

April 6
Emotional Energy Drain

One of the sneakiest sources of energy drain is our own emotions. Suppressed emotions cause invisible areas of buildup in our body and spirit, making us feel heavy and stuck. The first step to clearing the emotional buildup is to look your emotions in the face. When they start rising to the surface, don't suppress them. Instead, step back and observe the different layers of emotions. If you are feeling jealous, for example, look for the hidden emotion behind the jealousy.

April 7
The Power of Movement

Movement is the undercurrent of energy that animates all living things—even humans. Moving your body in gentle, rhythmic ways can help it to let go of stored emotions. I have experienced this in a very literal sense when I found myself crying at the end of a yoga class. It felt as though my heart was literally opening and years of suppressed pain was pouring out. You can release the emotional tension in your own body through yoga, dance, running, or even walking briskly in nature.

April 8
Reflection Questions

What would you do differently if you had double the energy you have now?

What emotions have you been suppressing or avoiding?

_____

_____

_____

_____

_____

_____

_____

April 9
EMOTIONAL FREEDOM

One of the best ways to release suppressed emotions is through Emotional Freedom Technique, otherwise known as EFT tapping. Like acupuncture, EFT stimulates the body's energy meridian points. It works with the natural energy channels in your body to heal and restore balance. I am not going to write an entire tutorial on EFT here because that's what YouTube is for. But I will emphasize a few key points:

- **Emotions are essential.** The more honest you can be about what you are feeling, the more effective EFT will be.
- **You don't have to do it perfectly.** EFT will work even if you aren't particularly precise or consistent.
- **You can make your own EFT affirmations.** Once you've watched some videos and you have a general sense of the flow, you can make up your own "negative" affirmations to release your specific fears and worries.

April 10

RELEASING THROUGH RITUAL

I am a strong believer in the power of ritual. That which we do symbolically on the outside creates real transformation on the inside. Here is a simple ritual to release emotional buildup:

Step 1: Write about the emotional trauma that is keeping you stuck. Detail what happened and what you wish had happened instead.

Step 2: Put on some sad music and mourn, baby, mourn.

Step 3: Write a goodbye letter to the person/place/feeling/experience, and then burn it.

April 11

AN INTROVERT'S HAPPY PLACE

For introverts, the right environment is key for creating the right state of mind. We need to find our own little introvert happy place where we can mentally recharge. In our happy place, there is probably something soft and cuddly—a blanket, an animal friend, a big comfy couch. there is also likely something that tickles our brain, such as music, art supplies, or a pen and paper. Let's be honest, Netflix is probably accessible, too. The next time you're feeling worn-down, go to your happy place and restore yourself, without guilt.

April 12
April Fortune Cookie

Let the fortune cookie decide your fate. Roll the dice, and read the fortune that coincides with the number you land on.

1. Loyalty is a virtue, but rigidity is its noose.
2. Your creative talents will open doors for you this week.
3. Your love life will be peaceful and harmonious.
4. You will reach your goal very soon.
5. A past love has been thinking of you lately.
6. Your character can be described as genuine and intriguing.

April 13
Building a Blanket Fortress

I know everyone has those days when they just want to hide out under a blanket rather than face the world. But, as introverts, I feel like we're a little more susceptible to these kinds of days. I must confess that there are many days when I stay swaddled in my blanket cocoon for as long as possible. I used to feel self-conscious about my bouts of extreme introverting, but I've learned to accept the natural ebb and flow of my energy. If you're having a hide-under-the-blankets kind of day, don't be too hard on yourself. Accept that part of living a balanced life is knowing that you will often be thrown off balance.

April 14

TAKING AN ELECTRONIC BREAK

We introverts are known for loving social media and all things Google. The Internet is a wonderland that feeds our ever-active mind. It also allows us to communicate by keystroke, which we <3. Even though our Internet escapades might seem like an escape from the sensory overload of the real world, our electronics can also be overstimulating. Give your brain a break by turning off your devices and focusing on relaxing tasks, such as cooking, drawing, grooming, writing in your journal, or just sitting in silence for a while.

April 15

MENTAL HEALTH DAY

In high school, I often felt exhausted. Even though I was a good student, I would occasionally skip school. While other kids played 'hooky' to go to the mall and see movies, I just wanted to take a nap. My mom and I had an understanding about my days off. We would call them "mental health days," and she was happy to write me a sick note. Nowadays, I have to write my own permission slips. I give myself a break, knowing that it is good for my mental and physical health. The next time you are feeling rundown, take a mental health day. Or at the very least, take a nap.

April 16

REFLECTION QUESTIONS

What is your introvert happy place? In other words, where do you go and what do you do to restore yourself and feel good?

What permission slip can you give yourself to restore your energy? Maybe your permission slip allows you to take a mental health day every now and then. Or perhaps it gives you the green light to make Sundays a day of rest.

_____

_____

_____

_____

_____

_____

_____

_____

_____

April 17
Bathing in the Dark

Taking a bath is both relaxing and rejuvenating for introverts because it provides an oasis of solitude. It is the reduction of stimulation that makes this activity so effective when you are feeling drained. Take your bath to the next level by creating a DIY sensory deprivation tank.

1. Fill your bathtub with lukewarm water and Epsom salt.
2. Block out sound and light with earplugs and an eye mask. You can also turn off the lights and just use a candle or nightlight.
3. Lie in your DIY sensory deprivation tank for up to one hour.

April 18
Walking Away Your Worries

Going for a walk is a great way to recharge because it connects you to nature, the ultimate source of rejuvenation. Research has shown that it also soothes the mind and prevents overthinking.

A Stanford study led by graduate student Gregory Bratman found that walking in nature quieted the part of the brain that is active during rumination. So, if you're feeling overwhelmed and depleted, go ahead and walk away your worries. Just be sure to stroll in a peaceful environment. If you live in a busy concrete jungle without a sliver of green in sight, try walking during a quiet time of day.

April 19

REPLENISHING CONNECTION

When you're feeling exhausted, you might be tempted to shut people out. After all, people are highly stimulating and, therefore, draining. But it's important to remember that it is the superficial relationships that introverts find most depleting. Emotionally intimate relationships that are built on acceptance rejuvenate you. When you're feeling depleted, you might need to be completely alone. Or you might need to curl up next to a loved one and let the warmth of human connection replenish you.

April 20

MONTHLY GRATITUDE MOMENT

Even with our energy woes, we introverts have much to be grateful for. Write down what you are most thankful for today. Your list might include relationships, material items, experiences, accomplishments, or opportunities. If you are particularly grateful for one thing, write more in-depth about it.

April 21

Running Away from Worries

Exercise might be the last thing you want to do when you are feeling depleted, but it is an amazing way to recharge as an introvert. In fact, going for nighttime runs was one of my main introvert coping strategies during high school. After a long day of classes, I would pop in my earbuds and run my worries away. If you're worried about making the trek to a gym after work, consider exercising at home or in your backyard. Working out at home saves you precious time, energy, and money.

April 22

Stretching Yourself

There is a form of exercise that provides mental, spiritual, and physical rejuvenation. Best of all, you can enjoy its replenishing effects by doing it for as little as five minutes a day. I am talking, of course, about yoga. I resisted doing yoga for a long time because it seemed boring and pointless, but last year I finally gave it a chance. Now I understand the hype. Doing yoga will help you feel grounded, focused, and rejuvenated. You don't even have to go to a class. Once you know the basic postures, you can do them anywhere. I even do back-release yoga in bed. Now that's what I call introvert-friendly exercise!

April 23

Reflection Questions

What is one easy and accessible way that you can allow in love and connection, even when you are feeling overwhelmed?

What part of your day is the most draining? Is there a way you can make it less depleting? For example, if the crowded subway zaps your energy during a morning commute, could you leave earlier a couple of days a week? If mornings feel chaotic, could you do more to prepare the night before?

_____

_____

_____

_____

_____

_____

_____

_____

_____

_____

_____

April 24

ARTISTIC EXPRESSION

Artistic expression is highly energizing for introverts. Your art has the power to get you out of bed in the morning and get you through a long day at work. It carries you home on a cloud as you anticipate reuniting with your creative projects. Make artistic expression a part of your daily routine, even if it doesn't seem practical—*especially* if it doesn't seem practical. That's the point, really. Art helps you escape the everyday mundane and create your own world.

April 25

MUSIC FOR YOUR SOUL

I'm a big believer in the power of resonance. When you find a song that reverberates within your soul and mind, you come back to life. Music soothes and mends what the workday leaves in pieces. If you're feeling rundown, put on some calming music, take a deep breath, and just sit back and listen for a while. You don't have to do anything else; listening is an activity in and of itself.

April 26
ENERGIZING FOODS

Food can have an enormous impact on an introvert's energy. Though everyone's dietary needs are different, many introverts are highly sensitive to certain foods and beverages. The wrong diet can leave you feeling foggy and lethargic. Try eliminating certain foods, particularly allergens (dairy, wheat, soy) and stimulants (coffee, alcohol, sugar) one at a time and see how you feel. Adding more fresh fruits and vegetables to your diet will also boost your energy. I personally follow a vegan diet and have found that this keeps my energy levels the most consistent.

April 27
JUST ENOUGH IS ENOUGH

Have you ever met someone who always has more than enough? They make more than enough food, give themselves more than enough time to get ready in the morning, and do more work than is necessary. I wonder how such people have the energy for more when I am always scraping by on just enough—just enough time, just enough work, just enough energy. And yet, an invisible cosmic force somehow transforms my feeble efforts into more than enough. I have been able to build a fulfilling life and business, despite always feeling like I should be doing more. I've realized that I don't need to be or do more because I am enough. As are you, my dear.

April 28
Energy Restoration Challenge

Adopt one of the energizing habits that I suggested in this month's entries for seven consecutive days. You might try going for nightly walks, doing some bedtime yoga, spending an hour away from electronics, or engaging in some form of artistic expression each day.

April 29
Go to Sleep

Since nighttime is usually the quietest time of day in any home, it is also when we introverts hear our own thoughts most clearly. When the lights go out, our brain turns on. This can make getting a good night's sleep difficult. Soothe your mind by turning off electronics an hour before bedtime. Meditating, doing yoga, and taking a bath will also help.

April 30
April Celebration

Don't wait until you reach the finish line to celebrate your life. There are tiny victories at every stage of the journey. Write down your celebration for this month, which can include any little bit of progress you've made or action steps you've taken, regardless of the outcome. Even just finishing reading a book, getting up earlier in the morning, or taking a beautiful photograph are accomplishments worth celebrating.

May

Blossoming

"And the day came when the risk to remain tight in a bud was more painful than the risk it took to blossom."
—Elizabeth Appell

May 1

GRASPING PASSION

As a teenager I spent a lot of time focused on self-betterment. Instead of looking forward to the next party, as many teens would, I looked forward to church events and student council meetings. I know that a lot of other introverts took a similar approach to surviving their teen years. Living in a structured, duty-oriented manner can take the edge off socializing. It is a way to be part of the excitement without getting lost in it.

But sometimes, you do want to lose yourself in the music and dance to the unexpected rhythms of life, but you don't know how. This was precisely my dilemma in the fall of 2003, my first year of university, when I wrote the below journal entry:

> I would like to be part of the color of life. I want my life to be a rich, vibrant painting, with many layers. I know this kind of life exists, but how do I get a hold on it? I picture myself dancing with eyes alight and a smile pressed upon my face. Or brimming with emotion as I watch and listen to the symphony. Where is my passion? I want to look up and LIVE!

My heart aches for this younger version of me. It was as though there was a big, beautiful party happening that she actually wanted to attend for once, but she didn't know how to get there. I love that she was willing to admit that she wanted more out of life. That is really the first step to getting what you want—actually admitting to yourself that you want it.

Looking back, I realize that I spent most of my twenties striving to be a part of that dazzling painting I described in my journal entry. I danced, traveled the world, went to parties, and made countless new friends. But in the end, I found the warm glow of passion I had been seeking within myself.

I have no regrets about my duty-filled teens or my passion-driven twenties. I recognize that every moment of searching and striving was a chance to blossom into the woman I am today. Most importantly, I know that I don't need to chase a brightly painted horizon for fulfillment. The spark of life is within me. This month's entries will help you find your own inner spark and blossom into your authentic self.

May 2

CREATING THE RIGHT CONDITIONS

Not all flowers blossom when and where you want them to. Some plants can only grow under certain conditions. They need just the right mix of sun and shade, wind and rain. It is the same for introverts. Often, we simply can't blossom in the soil where we have been planted. To truly come into our own, we need to seek out more solitude and less constant busyness; more meaning and less going through the motions. We must also know that it's okay to ask for what we need. Sometimes, it feels like the world wants us to wither—it expects us to! But we are meant to stand tall and find our nourishment from within.

May 3

BUILDING WITHOUT A BLUEPRINT

People think that transformation, and change in general, is a hard stop, the edge of a cliff at the end of a sentence. But a transformation is more like a series of commas and semicolons. It is a run-on sentence in the story of your life; a long winding question, rather than a definite answer. You are becoming. But that doesn't mean you have any idea what the hell you're doing or where you'll end up. You must build without a blueprint and trust that it will all come together in the end.

May 4

MAY BOOK NOOK

Here are some book recommendations to help you blossom as an introvert.

1. *The Perks of Being a Wallflower* by Stephen Chbosky
2. *White Oleander: A Novel* by Janet Fitch
3. *The Girl with the Lower Back Tattoo* by Amy Schumer
4. *The Introvert's Way: Living a Quiet Life in a Noisy World* by Sophia Dembling
5. *Eat Pray Love Made Me Do It: Life Journeys Inspired by the Bestselling Memoir* by various authors

May 5

Noticing the Small Things

Be mindful of the small things today that could mean something big for tomorrow. Someone once told me that if I see a penny on the ground, I should always pick it up—not for good luck, but as a way of telling my subconscious and the universe that I notice and appreciate money. Today, I am picking up a penny, but tomorrow I could just as easily be receiving much more. The same philosophy applies to love, friendship, and purpose. Look up, and notice the little gestures and signs that could be pointing toward something bigger.

May 6

Blooming Bravely

Make no mistake, blossoming into your authentic self is a risk, and it will feel terrifying at times. You risk rejection, disappointment, embarrassment. Even the prospect of shining is a risk. You feel self-conscious of your power, as if it is wrong to be aware of your strength. Indeed, it takes courage to be the quiet flower that blooms in spite of fear. But it is worth it.

May 7

WHAT WOULD YOUR LITTLE OLD LADY SELF DO?

This might surprise you, but sometimes we introverts get the urge to do things that aren't very "introvert like." This is exactly what happened to me at a local festival a while ago. While listening to a reggae band, I had the sudden urge to dance. But no one else was dancing, besides an elderly woman, who bobbed away freely to the beats. I thought to myself, *One day I'll be one of those little old ladies who dances like no one's watching.* Then I wondered why I wouldn't give myself permission to dance that way now. I started asking myself, *What would my little old lady self do?* It's a great question to ask when you are questioning your heart's desires.

May 8

REFLECTION QUESTIONS

Do you feel like the world is making you wither? What do you need more of or less of to blossom today?

What is the desire that you are trying to suppress? What would your little old lady self tell you to do?

_____

_____

_____

_____

_____

May 9

Stop Abandoning Yourself

Transformation brings up a lot of memories and feelings you might rather avoid. If you feel an uncomfortable emotion coming on, sit with it for a while instead of running away. Even if someone decides to leave you in the most painful way or you feel like God has forgotten you. Hold your ground. Stay with you.

May 10

Give It All Away

It is time to give away the thing that is not meant for you: the hectic job, the overstuffed social calendar, the lover who doesn't love you back, the need to please, the extrovert's blueprint for a fulfilling life—give it up, so you can reclaim YOU.

May 11

Make Lists

Make lists to help you blossom. I don't mean to-do lists. Fill pages with reasons why you're loveable. Make a gratitude list, a desire list, a list of every nice thing anyone's ever said to you. Make a list of things that make you angry, things you know to be true, things you should have learned by now.

May 12

MAY FORTUNE COOKIE

Let the fortune cookie decide your fate. Roll the dice, and read the fortune that coincides with the number you land on.

1. You will take a chance on something new very soon.
2. You will receive a happy surprise in the mail in the near future.
3. You will soon make a career change.
4. Your friends look to you for wise counsel.
5. You are almost there.
6. You are an old soul.

May 13

No More Time for Longing

There is no more time
for longing.
I am a grown woman,
if I have a dream
I take it between my teeth
like a mama lion
and I say,
Here.
You must exist now.

If you are a dreamer like me, you know how easy it is to live inside your fantasies. But it's never good to fall asleep in pretend worlds. That's how your real life gets away from you.

Unspoken dreams are the most dangerous because we might not even realize that they are there until we feel the holes they tear in our soul as they pass us by. If you have a dream, take it between your teeth and bring it into reality. Command it to exist, or set it free.

May 14

Slowing Down

Speeding through is the extrovert's way. We introverts are happier when we take the scenic route in life. I used to be in a terrible rush to grow my business quickly, but now I am grateful that I wasn't an overnight success. I see that I needed time to grow my inner toolkit so that I could handle the responsibilities and stresses that come with each new level of success. Slow down and take your time—the finish line keeps moving until you're dead; so, you see, there is really no need to rush.

May 15

MEASURING BY EMOTIONS

Measure your life by emotions instead of achievements. If something made you feel strong, happy, alive, excited, or better than you were before, that is worth celebrating. Your emotions will also help you to edit your life. You'll know something doesn't belong if it feels heavy, like a lie. Or if thinking about it makes your stomach turn.

May 16

REFLECTION QUESTIONS

Does change scare you? What small action step could you take to make change less daunting?

Has a word, place, or person been popping up again and again in unexpected ways? Don't pass it off as coincidence. Take note of it, and consider what message life is trying to send you.

_____

_____

_____

_____

_____

_____

_____

May 17

INTROVERSION IS NOT A LIMITATION

As you blossom into your authentic self, don't hold yourself back by thinking that your introversion is a limitation. You can be a social introvert, an adventurous introvert, or a wild introvert. Introverts share many traits and challenges, but we are still each unique. And every one of us has the capacity to live an extraordinary life.

May 18

YOU WILL RISE

Are you having a hard time right now? Is your life more struggle than sunshine? When you're at your lowest, it can be hard to see the purpose of your pain. But if you look back at your darkest hours, you'll see that these were the moments when your life was changing because *you* were changing. Often, it takes hitting rock bottom to finally stop resisting your own transformation. It is a relief to feel the cold, hard earth catch you and to know that you will no longer run. You will rise.

May 19

A Fresh Chance

As humans, we are drawn to transformation stories. We love seeing before and after photos or watching a makeover story unfold before our eyes. Lately, I have been utterly mesmerized by a YouTube beauty guru named Nikkie who does makeup tutorials on her channel, "NikkieTutorials." I don't even try to mimic her looks; I just love watching her apply her makeup and seeing what a difference each layer makes. I'm equally addicted to transformations in my own life. Every inner transformation provides a blank canvas, a fresh chance to create my world. If change seems scary to you, try thinking of it as a fresh opportunity to turn the page on your own makeover story.

May 20

Monthly Gratitude Moment

What better way is there to live life than to wake up every morning with thank you on your lips and go to sleep with gratitude in your heart? Take a moment to write down what you are most grateful for today. Your list can be abundant and include all the little things you adore. Or you could write in-depth about one thing that really lights up your heart with gratitude.

May 21

My Before and After

My "before" story:

When I was younger, I was like a lot of introverts who feel like they don't fit in. I constantly worried that there was something wrong with me. I felt ashamed of my personality and thought that if I could just fix my flaws, I'd be worthy of love and happiness. I also felt a deep sense of loneliness. It was the kind of loneliness you only experience when you feel like you don't belong and never will.

My dramatic "after":

Learning to embrace my introversion has changed my life in many unexpected ways. I listen more to my intuition and care less about what other people think. I also feel less guilty as I extend more compassion toward myself. Overall, I feel that I am living with more purpose and authenticity.

If you feel like you're still in the "before" part of your story, consider this your invitation to join me on the "after" side. I think you'll like it here.

May 22

Be One of the Strange Ones

Many introverts deny their greatest strengths in an effort to fit in. They trade in extraordinary for just plain ordinary. But a lot of the most exceptional people in this world are introverts. They are the outliers who don't fit in—and who don't want to. They are the dreamers, the artists, the strange ones. So why not embrace your strange and extraordinary self? Who knows what will happen. Surely, nothing short of magic.

Trust the Inner Pull

Be brave enough to wade into the quietness you crave as an introvert. Wisdom comes to those who create the space to hear their inner voice. Your solitude has secrets to share with you. Trust the messages you receive during quiet reflection, knowing that the path of authenticity isn't always logical. You can take the first steps without seeing the entire staircase.

May 24

Reflection Questions

If you feel like you are in the "before" part of your transformation, take a moment to imagine what your "after" will look and feel like.

How can you embrace your strangeness and be more of who you truly are today?

_____

_____

_____

_____

_____

_____

_____

May 25

Embrace Your Inner Boldness

A lot of people have this preconceived idea that all introverts are timid wallflowers who speak in whispered tones and tiptoe through life. While we may be quiet and calm, many introverts have an inner boldness that comes out in our passions. Embrace your fierceness, even if it seems at odds with your "gentle" introvert nature. You are allowed to shatter people's expectations, especially your own.

May 26

Figuring It Out as You Go

Life can be confusing as an introvert. People give you mixed messages, saying things like "be yourself," and then doling out advice about how to come out of your shell. You wonder how you can get all the things you want in life while feeling so different from everyone else. The truth is that no one knows what the hell they are doing. The problem is not the fact that you haven't got it all figured out. It's that you feel like you should.

May 27

You've Already Arrived

Life is not a happy ending. It's so much else, but it just isn't that. If you are still waiting to arrive, know that you already have. Wherever you are and whatever your circumstances, you are in the process of creating your life story. Every chapter has its purpose. Stop worrying about the conclusion and make this chapter meaningful.

May 28

Blossoming Challenge

Create a dream board. You can either use Google Photos to do this or old magazines.

Step 1: Cut out pictures that represent your most important goals for this year. You can include business, relationship, travel, and health goals.

Step 2: Glue the pictures to your board or digitally create a collage using Google Photos and save it as your desktop background.

Step 3: Every night this week, look at each picture for 1 to 2 minutes and vividly imagine how it would *feel* to have that thing. Really bask in the emotions as if you are already there.

May 29

Feel Your Way There

Being an INFP personality type, I usually make decisions based on feelings. When people ask me why I decided to make a drastic change in life, such as moving cities or wandering the earth for a year, I try to give them some sort of logical answer. But the truth is simply that my body told me to do it. I was listening to my heart, gut, bones, and some deep longing in my womb. I didn't do it because it made sense; I did it because I've learned that ignoring my intuition leads to a life of pain—long-lasting, expensive, and secret—the kind of pain you hide behind a face you no longer recognize. I like being able to look myself in the mirror and be at peace with my decisions. I've found that feeling my way through life is the only way to achieve this.

A Sea of Possibilities

About eight years ago, when I was separating from my then-husband, we had a teary goodbye conversation on a rocky beach. As I looked out at the shimmering sea before me, a little voice inside me made a promise I will never forget. It said that this would be my life—an endless sea of possibility and beauty. So, I needn't mourn for what I was leaving behind. Now, I have seen that promise fulfilled a thousand times over, both literally and figuratively. Every day, I wake up and see that same ocean, and I know that this is only the beginning. As you go through difficult transitions, remember that there is a sea of possibility before you and that this could be the start of something beautiful.

May Celebration

There are tiny buds of possibility emerging in your life, I just know it. Take a moment to think about what you would like to celebrate today. What small triumph do you want to revisit and write about in your journal? Remember, your celebrations can be simple, everyday things. Sometimes, just getting out of bed in the morning and facing the day is worth celebrating.

June

Connection Equations

"I talked to a calzone for fifteen minutes last night before I realized it was just an introverted pizza. I wish all my acquaintances were so tasty."
—Jarod Kintz, *This Book Has No Title*

June 1

Introvert Conversations

"Introverts crave meaning, so party chitchat feels like sandpaper to our psyche."
—Diane Cameron, "Happy Introvert Day,"
The Christian Science Monitor

People tend to think that introverts don't want to connect with others. Because we are quiet, they assume we have nothing to share. This couldn't be further from the truth. We want to have interesting conversations and make meaningful friendships, but sometimes we don't know how.

We can't seem to get past our communication obstacles, such as our tendency toward speaking slowly and pausing often. We would rather be like the fast-talking extroverts, whom everyone seems to like. But we needn't get discouraged.

Confident communication is a skill like any other. In the same way that you can learn to read and play music, you can learn to be a great conversationalist. For introverts, the key components for communication mastery are already there: we have the intellect, self-awareness, listening skills, and observation skills. This month's entries will help you tap into your communication strengths and start making connections in your own introverted way.

June 2

Savoring Sentences

I have a friend who is a great talker. She tells long and detailed stories punctuated with enthusiasm and humor. I'll admit that it is a pleasure to be around such a vivacious conversationalist. She's a streak of red in an otherwise grey day. But I also enjoy the kinds of conversations that feel more like a leisurely swim through calm waters. I could spend all afternoon savoring these slower paced, but more in-depth, conversations. If you feel self-conscious about your slow-talking ways, remember that introvert conversations can be delicious even if they lack that extroverted punch of gregariousness.

June 3

Far from Boring

"What I wonder is why would anyone want to be friends with us introverts? We're so boring." This was the question posed by a man I met at an introvert retreat a while ago. The interesting thing is that he said it in a matter-of-fact way, as if the words "introvert" and "boring" were an expected pairing. But introverts are far from boring. We have unique ideas, passions, and perspectives—a whole world of interesting things to share. We simply need to bridge the gap between what we think, believe, and dream, and what we say.

June 4

June Book Nook

Here is are some books to help you connect with your fellow humanoids.

1. *The Like Switch: An Ex-FBI Agent's Guide to Influencing, Attracting, and Winning People Over* by Jack Schafer, PhD
2. *The Fine Art of Small Talk: How to Start a Conversation, Keep It Going, Build Networking Skills—and Leave a Positive Impression!* by Debra Fine
3. *The Irresistible Introvert: Harness the Power of Quiet Charisma in a Loud World* by Michaela Chung (you didn't expect me to not plug my other book, did you?)
4. *The Art of Asking: How I Learned to Stop Worrying and Let People Help* by Amanda Palmer
5. *The Introvert Advantage: How Quiet People Can Thrive in an Extrovert World* by Marti Olsen Laney, PsyD

June 5

BE A GIVER

Introverts often approach interactions with what I call a "beggar's mindset." We assume that we are taking something from the other person by engaging them in conversation. Remember that you are not a beggar, but rather, a giver. The gifts you offer are your ear, your presence, and your curiosity. You also offer connection points, little specks of shared experiences and emotion that make people feel less alone.

June 6

CONSIDERATE CONVERSATIONS

I personally love talking to fellow introverts because they know how to slow down in conversation. They don't pounce at the edges of all my sentences, eager to share their own thoughts before I have the chance to finish mine. I like the pauses, the steady flow, the sincerity. Likewise, others will appreciate your more thoughtful and considerate way of communicating.

June 7

SOCIAL ENERGY CYCLES

Introverts have a limited amount of juice in our social batteries. Once they are depleted, conversations come to a screeching halt—or at least we wish they would. Sometimes, we force ourselves to talk long after our energy levels have reached empty. At this point we might shut down and start to zone out mid-conversation. Honor your introvert needs by politely excusing yourself from conversations when you feel your batteries getting low.

June 8

REFLECTION QUESTIONS

Why do you enjoy talking to your favorite conversation partners? What is it about their body language, tone, and the way they approach conversations that you find enjoyable?

What are some things that you wish you could share in conversation? What's holding you back from doing so?

_____

_____

_____

_____

_____

_____

June 9

LIMIT THE MEET AND GREET

Interacting with strangers compounds our sense of depletion. In get-to-know-you conversations, there is so much information to process before we even open our mouth. We are simultaneously listening, watching for body language cues, and trying to act natural. Make things easier for yourself by setting a time limit on a meet and greet. Tell yourself that you will talk to new people for the first thirty minutes of an event, and then you will allow yourself to sit back and observe or talk with a close friend.

June 10

UNLEASH YOUR BRILLIANCE

"Keep your stupid on a leash." I heard this charming little Southern idiom while watching a movie the other day. It puts a playful spin on some pretty brash advice: stop doing and saying dumb things. As introverts, we tend to keep our stupid on a very tight leash. We put a lot of thought into what we do and don't say. The problem is that we are so afraid of saying the wrong thing that we end up putting our brilliance on a leash, too. Try loosening the leash a little and letting more of yourself out in conversation, even if that means saying the wrong thing every now and then.

June 11

The Power of Subtlety

There is a misconception in our culture that bigger personalities always win and that making friends requires that you be loud and gregarious. For introverts, this feels unnatural. To connect in a way that feels more authentic, try on a little subtlety for size. Remember that subtle changes lead to big results.

Here are some ideas:

- Instead of forcing a big smile, try smiling with your eyes.
- Instead of talking louder, just enunciate your words more.
- Instead of power posing, try straightening your neck and relaxing your shoulders.

June 12

June Fortune Cookie

Let the fortune cookie decide your fate. Roll the dice, and read the fortune that coincides with the number you land on.

1. Your patience will be tested today.
2. The best way to predict the future is to invent it.
3. Your intuition will guide you toward great riches.
4. The events are unfolding to bring your soulmate to you.
5. The best prediction of the future is the past.
6. You will find what you were looking for sitting right next to you.

June 13

Close Friends vs. Strangers

Introverts tend to find it much easier to open up with close friends and family. Only a select few get to see our secret playful side or delight in our unexpected sense of humor. While acquaintances assume we're just quiet wallflowers, our best friends know we are beautifully complex. Remember, there is nothing wrong with being selective with whom you truly open up to, as long as you're letting someone in.

June 14

Inner Dialogue

There is one person with whom introverts can always have a lively conversation, and that is ourself. An introvert's mental chatter can out-talk any daytime talk show. Our internal conversations keep us entertained, but it's more than that. Because introverts process more information at a given time than extroverts, our internal dialogue becomes a way of untangling what we take in. So, keep talking to yourself; it's how you make sense of the world.

June 15
SAYING MORE WITH LESS

"I am a minimalist. I like saying the most with the least."
—Bob Newhart, *I Shouldn't Even Be Doing This:*
And Other Things That Strike Me as Funny

Introverts are often self-conscious about how little we say. But word economy is not the enemy in introvert conversations. What matters most is that you are able to get the true meaning of your message past the editor and into the airspace between you and your partner. Saying more with less is what will lead to true connection.

June 16
REFLECTION QUESTIONS

What will be your time limit for a meet and greet at your next social event? Thinking about how long it usually takes you to start zoning out at a party will help you decide. How would your best friend describe you?

_____

_____

_____

_____

_____

_____

June 17
Untying Your Tongue

Have you ever wanted desperately to keep a conversation going but couldn't think of a single thing to say? Getting tongue-tied is one of the biggest challenges introverts face, but it doesn't have to be that way. You can fill pregnant pauses by making an observation, and then getting curious about what you see.

There are four main types of observations you can make:

- **Make an observation about the environment:** "Your garden looks amazing. I'm thinking of starting my own garden. Do you have any advice?"
- **Make an observation about your partner:** "That's a unique bracelet. Is there a story behind it?"
- **Make an observation about other people (keep it positive or neutral):** "Nancy is such a great hostess. I wish I had her ability to multitask. Do you host many parties?"
- **Make an observation about your own feelings:** "That speech really inspired me. How did you feel about it?"

June 18
Anticipating Awkwardness

One of the best ways to feel more relaxed in conversation is to accept that awkwardness is normal—and also temporary. Embrace it as part of the process, and you'll find the awkwardness dissipating more quickly than you imagined. My motto is: "Just because it starts out awkward, doesn't mean it has to stay that way." Give every conversation the three-minute rule. If it doesn't feel more natural after three minutes, you can politely excuse yourself.

June 19

A Sense of Belonging

I have a friend who likes to sneak into the members-only lounge at airports. When I asked her how she does it without a membership card, she shrugged her shoulders and replied, "When you act like you belong somewhere, people assume that you do." Remember, if you've been invited to a place, you belong there, flaws and all.

June 20

Monthly Gratitude Moment

What relationships are you most grateful for? Your list can include people who have only touched your life for a brief time or current family members, colleagues, and friends. If you wish, write down some of the reasons you appreciate each relationship.

June 21

Setting Connection Micro Goals

It's easy for introverts to lose heart as we struggle to make new friends. The best way to stay motivated is to set an achievable connection goal. "Achievable" is really the operative word here. If you expect every social event to yield lifelong friends, you will lose heart quickly. Setting micro goals will keep you motivated. Before you know it, you will be making true friends, without exhaustion and anxiety. Here are some examples of micro goals:

- Initiating conversation with at least one new person
- Smiling (genuinely) at three people
- Practicing one connection tip from this book

June 22

Connecting Close to Home

Studies have shown that proximity, the simple act of being near another person on a regular basis, increases the chances of friendship. This is one of the reasons we tend to bond with coworkers, classmates, and teammates, even if we seem to have little in common. If you want to make new friends, look to the places you visit most regularly, such as work and school, as a starting point. If those seem fruitless, try a new activity that you can do on a consistent basis.

June 23

Staying Motivated

Because socializing is so draining for introverts, the idea of making new friends isn't always enough motivation to get us out of the house. That's why it helps to dangle another carrot in front of your nose. You can do this by choosing activities you would want to do regardless of whether you think you'll meet interesting people or not. I've made most of my close friends through my passions and spiritual pursuits, such as salsa dancing, church, New Age groups, and traveling.

June 24

REFLECTION QUESTIONS

What is a reasonable connection micro goal that you can set for your next social event?

How can you use one of your passions to connect with people?

_____

_____

_____

June 25

QUALITY OVER QUANTITY

"I'm very picky with whom I give my energy to. I prefer to reserve my time, intensity and spirit exclusively to those who reflect sincerity."

—Dau Voire

Introverts are hardwired to value quality over quantity in relationships. We want fewer friends but deeper connections. Growing up, I always had one best friend with whom I spent nearly all my free time. To this day, I prefer to have a tight-knit friend circle. Though I have many friends spread far and wide all over the world, in my day-to-day life, I pour most of my social energy into two or three close friends. I share this because people often think that you need to juggle a lot of friends and social activities to feel fulfilled. When it comes to making friends as an introvert, quality really is more important than quantity.

June 26

Equal Heroes

Many introverts find it easier to make friends with extroverts because they are more likely to reach out and carry the conversation. As you get closer, you might begin putting your extroverted friend on a pedestal. You imagine that they are superior because they are more popular. Just for the record, your extroverted friend is not the hero of your story. You are not the Robin to his Batman, or the floundering fish to her mermaid. You are different, but equal.

June 27

Befriending Fellow Introverts

Even if we want to make friends with other introverts, sometimes we simply don't know how. We wonder who will make the first move. Will we have anything to talk about? As you probably already know, we introverts appreciate when someone else takes the lead in establishing a friendship. We also value persistence and loyalty. If you can reach out to a fellow introvert and stick around, despite a bit of awkwardness, he or she may warm to you surprisingly quickly. Of course, it is worth the effort, because there is nothing like having an introvert on your side in life.

June 28

Connection Challenge

Reach out to someone you don't normally hang out with and make plans to meet. This could be someone you used to be friends with or an acquaintance you would like to get to know better. Choose someone who seems open and kind and who will likely welcome your invitation.

June 29

Opening Up

Opening up can be tough for introverts. We remember all the times we tried to open up but were interrupted by someone louder and more gregarious. We also have a secret fear of rejection, which we expertly hide beneath a mask of aloofness. The secret to opening up as an introvert is to take a step-by-step approach. Gradually share more about who you are and what's important to you. Your personal preferences are a great place to start. Go ahead and share your likes and dislikes without invitation. Later, you can share relevant stories and experiences. Eventually you'll feel comfortable being more vulnerable and sharing your deepest fears and dreams.

June 30

June Celebration

You made it through the long cold days of winter and the fog of spring, and now summer is here! That in itself is something to celebrate. What other step in the right direction, great or small, would you like to celebrate today?

July

LESSONS IN LONELINESS

"If you are the type of person who thinks too much about stuff then there is nothing lonelier in the world than being surrounded by a load of people on a different wavelength."
—Matt Haig, *Reasons to Stay Alive*

July 1

The Way Out of Loneliness

If loneliness were a place, it would be the most frequently visited, as well as the most secretive, place in the world. Everyone has felt lonely at some point in their life, but few admit to it.

The very word *lonely* drips with shame. We feel the need to hide our loneliness and pretend that everything is okay. For introverts, especially, there is a sense of pressure to deal with loneliness the same way that we deal with everything else: in isolation. But when it comes to loneliness, our fierce independence gets the better of us. Trying to solve the problem of loneliness on our own is like trying to play patty cake without a partner. It simply doesn't work.

So, what is the solution? How do we "cure" chronic loneliness? For many introverts, this question is more complicated than it appears. We need our alone time to feel our best. And yet, we also need human connection to stay happy and fulfilled. How can we balance these two innate needs when they so often seem at odds with one another?

Loneliness is not as invincible, nor is it as shameful, as it appears. Once you admit that you are lonely, it is like bringing the Boogie Monster into the light of day. Loneliness loses its power when you look it in the face and recognize that you are bigger, stronger, and—if we're being honest—much better looking than it could ever hope to be. This month's entries will help you to leave loneliness behind and find a happy balance between solitude and connection.

July 2

SOLITUDE VS. LONELINESS

Loneliness expresses the pain of being alone and solitude expresses the glory of being alone.
—Paul Tillich, *The Eternal Now*

Alone and lonely are not the same thing, or at least, they don't need to be. For introverts, solitude can be a sweet sanctuary, offering nourishment for the mind and soul. But too much time alone can sour the sweetness of solitude. Loneliness is the bitter aftertaste of expired solitude. Avoiding the sting of loneliness is a matter of knowing the shelf life of your particular brand of solitude. For some introverts, an entire day alone is too much; for others, it is not enough. Sometimes, you can extend the vitality of your solitude by adding the right ingredients—an animal friend, a walk in the forest, a thick and delicious book. The important thing is to avoid sabotaging your solitude by worrying that you should be doing something else. You can have your slice of solitude and enjoy it, too. And when it's time to come up for air, you can return rejuvenated to the people you care about.

July 3
Feeling a Sense of Urgency

As humans, we so easily take time for granted. We tell ourselves that we'll learn how to open up and reach out another day, another week, another year. It's no wonder that the most difficult changes emerge from urgency. An unexpected event, such as a breakup, death, or close call, forces us to stop procrastinating our transformation. We vow to change—not next year, not when we have more money, not after we reach our career goals—but right now. Luckily, you don't have to go through a tragedy to find your way out of loneliness. I've found that one question really helps to put things in perspective:

If you continue on as you are without making any significant changes to shift your loneliness, what will your life look like one year from now? And how does that make you feel?

July 4
July Book Nook

1. *When Breath Becomes Air* by Paul Kalanithi
2. *On Living* by Kerry Egan
3. *True Love: A Practice for Awakening the Heart* by Thich Nhat Hanh
4. *The Ocean at the End of the Lane: A Novel* by Neil Gaiman
5. *The Tao of Pooh* by Benjamin Hoff

July 5

Enjoying Alone

There is a myth that introverts always enjoy being alone. The truth is that sometimes we are so busy feeling guilty and self-conscious about our aloneness that we can't enjoy it. I've noticed that when I start comparing myself to my more extroverted friends, my once lovely alone time gets swallowed up by guilt. I start to feel lonely, but it is not because I am alone; it is because I am not allowing myself to enjoy my solitude. On the other hand, when I sink into my solitude and immerse myself in a creative project, I barely notice I'm alone. The next time you feel lonely, push your guilt aside and focus on a creative project or passion.

July 6

Quieting the "Should" Voice

Our alone time is often soured by what I call the "Should" voice. This is the voice that reminds us of all the productive things we should be doing instead of enjoying our solitude. Perhaps, the "Should" voice tells you that you should be out with friends or running errands, instead of sitting at home alone. The next time it emerges, imagine it as a shrill and high-pitched mouse. Now pick up the annoying little rodent by the tail and toss him out the door. If he tries to return, remind him that you are much bigger than him, and he'd best keep his tiny mouth shut if he knows what's good for him.

July 7

GROWING IN SOLITUDE

One of the greatest gifts of introversion is the ability to discover the many treasures hidden within solitude. Our alone time helps us to reconnect with our intuition, become more self-aware, integrate our experiences, and gain wisdom. Take a moment to reflect on how being alone has made you a better person.

July 8

REFLECTION QUESTIONS

How does your "Should" voice prevent you from enjoying solitude?

What are your favorite solo creative activities? Can you make an effort to do more of them this week?

_____

_____

_____

_____

_____

_____

_____

_____

_____

July 9

PLANNING AHEAD

For introverts, it can be hard to know where the line is between blissful solitude and heart-wrenching loneliness. I can go two days straight without seeing a single human being, but by the third day, I yearn for connection. Loneliness saps motivation, so once it takes hold, I might not have the will to reach out. That's why it's essential for introverts to plan ahead. For me, this means scheduling two to three social activities for the week ahead. I also recommend having weekly social events that you can count on no matter what: a book club meeting, Friday night drinks with your best friend, Sunday dinner with the family, game night, etc.

July 10

GETTING A HEAD START

Loneliness rarely storms in unannounced. Usually its arrival is no surprise at all. If loneliness were a person, she would send you texts every few hours to remind you of your upcoming date. In real life, loneliness warns you of its arrival through your feelings and thoughts. You start to feel bored, lethargic, and unmotivated. Your thoughts go from constructive to critical, as you find more and more reasons to feel sorry for yourself. As soon as you notice the warning signs, start reaching out and grasping for any branch of hope you can find. Make plans with friends, join a gym, call someone, take up a new hobby, or revisit an old passion. Do whatever it takes to keep the loneliness from engulfing you.

July 11

AN OFFERING OF HOPE

I wrote the poem below when I was drowning in the depths of loneliness. It was a tree branch of hope that I grasped with both hands. I
hope it helps you to find your way out of dark times.

The Shape of Love

I used to think that love was the shape of a paper heart
And the weight of a body on my body,
It could be contained in a puff of white air on a winter night
Or in the space of a mouth on my mouth.
For a while I thought love was the shape of a church steeple,
If I just stepped inside one of these glowing buildings
I could take as much love home with me as I needed,
But love was like sand disappearing through the cracks in my hands.
When I was little, love fit so nicely in my mother's arms and my
*   father's hands,*
Even my mean older brother had some love hidden between his toes,
But then my family spread like five fingers reaching for a thousand
*   stars*
And so did love.
Love was on the other end of an invisible cord,
It was inside the square of my computer screen.
Love had a tight schedule,
It could only fit you in on weekends, birthdays, holidays,
When it was lonely or going through a breakup.
Now I think it's funny that I thought I was the sculptor
And love would take the shape I told it to.
I actually believed that I could trim love down to the size of a paper
*   heart,*
Make it the weight of a body on my body,

Contain it in the space of a mouth on my mouth,
But sometimes love is so gigantic it frightens me
Or so small and secret I can't even see it.
The other day I noticed that love curls perfectly around the "O" in HOPE.
Hope is like a down payment on love,
It says, "I can't afford you now, but I got plans, baby"
When love seems unseeable and impossible
Hope is a candle between two mirrors
Sending love in a hundred different directions—
No, sending love from a hundred different directions.
Hope is a puff of white air returning to my lungs
And teaching me how to breathe again,
It says, even though I don't know the shape and weight of love today,
Tomorrow love could be five fingers holding a thousand stars
At the same time that it holds my hand,
It might be the shape of a sanctuary
And the weight of two feet straddling your world and mine.
Someone once told me that children are hope.
My womb has never produced anything but words
So I choose to be my own child
And I tell her, baby, love probably isn't the shape of a paper heart
Or the weight of a body on your body,
You are not love's sculptor.
All this time you thought you were shaping love,
Love has been shaping you.

July 12

JULY FORTUNE COOKIE

Let the fortune cookie decide your fate. Roll the dice, and read the fortune that coincides with the number you land on.

1. When you become too much, it is the same as not being enough.
2. You will dazzle your guest with your fine hosting skills.
3. Tonight, you will be blinded by passion.
4. You will face a situation where you will have to assert yourself.
5. Someone special will show you that they care.
6. There is no such thing as an ordinary cat.

July 13

MAKE A MANIFESTO

Make a manifesto that will be your guiding light the moment you feel loneliness creeping in. Let the words be a declaration of all the reasons you have to keep fighting for your own happiness. Include your core values, purpose, goals, and dreams. It helps to split your manifesto into sections: I am, I want, I will. I'll share examples of each section in the next three days' entries.

July 14

I AM . . .

A creator, seeker, poet, artist, introvert, sensitive soul, giver of hope, bearer of beauty, dancer, lover, fighter, truth seeker, friend, daughter, sister, flawed human, strong woman, hopeful romantic, peaceful adventurer, goddess, siren.

Your turn! Write an "I am" statement of your own. You can be as literal or poetic as you like.

July 15

I WANT . . .

To live to see my legacy take root, to be beautiful when I'm one hundred, to listen more than I speak, to make poetry out of every tragedy, to love more and fear less. I want to wake up every morning with "thank you" on my lips, sing like no one's listening, and dance like God is watching. I want to be myself without apology, shape my life however I choose, write a new story, and let go of the chapters that no longer fit. I want to sleep on the moon and dance with the stars.

Your turn! Write an "I want" statement of your own.

July 16
I WILL . . .

Keep going so that I can express myself creatively, give what only I can give, and live a life of meaning and purpose. I will tell the truth, be authentic, and have the difficult conversations. I will choose love, even when it is scary. I will see the world from as many different perspectives as possible, and live to write about it. I will never pretend to be someone I'm not. I will love and accept myself no matter what.

Your turn! Write an "I will" statement of your own.

July 17
REFLECTION QUESTIONS

Write down the names of the people you would like to connect with in the coming week, and send them a text or email to set it up.

Take a moment to write down some potential weekly social activities that you could commit to (and enjoy).

_____

_____

_____

_____

_____

_____

July 18

SEEING THE EMPTY SPACES

At times, there can be a certain comfort to loneliness. You settle into it as if it were a well-worn pair of jeans. But then you meet someone who makes you acutely aware of your loneliness. The warmth of their presence makes way for a stabbing absence the moment they leave. It's as if they flicked a switch inside you, and now you can see all the holes in your existence, the empty spaces that only another human can fill. It is possible for this feeling to fade. The holes can close up, the heart can toughen, the walls around your world can stand tall once more. But is that really what you want?

July 19

PROTECTING YOURSELF

Sometimes, no matter how much we crave the warmth of human connection, our behavior says otherwise. We come off as cold and aloof. Really, the more appropriate word is "self-protective." Even though we're lonely, we keep others at arm's length to protect ourselves from being overwhelmed or drained of energy. Our methods for keeping others at a distance can be very effective. So effective, in fact, that we find ourselves stuck in a chronic cycle of loneliness and longing. It's natural to be self-protective as an introvert. But it's also important to remember to set down your armor every now and then and put out a welcome sign.

July 20

Monthly Gratitude Moment

When you are in the depths of loneliness and despair, it's hard to find the strength to say thank you. But doing so can provide a way out of the darkness. Write down whatever you can think of to be grateful for today. If you can only think of one thing, write at length about it.

July 21

Feeling Misunderstood

Introverts often feel misunderstood. We are used to being surrounded by people who are on a different wavelength than us. We don't identify with them anymore than they do us, and this is, perhaps, the loneliest feeling of all. Thankfully, all it takes is one person who truly understands us—or even just understands one important aspect of us— to feel like we're not so alone after all. Chances are such a person already exists in your life. Reach out to them and make plans to meet.

July 22

Leaving the Crowd

What do you do when you feel lonelier in a crowded room than when you are alone? First of all, know that it's okay to feel out of place in crowds. Introverts find fulfillment and friendship in quieter spaces, such as being tucked away in quirky coffee shops, cozy artists' gatherings, or lush fields blooming with gentle people. Don't waste time on social activities that are devoid of true connection. Ask yourself: Can I be myself and have a meaningful conversation at this event? If the answer is no, it might not be worth your time.

July 23

Feeling Lonely in a Relationship

The loneliness you experience when you are in a relationship with the wrong person can be the most painful loneliness of all. There is nothing more heartbreaking than sitting across from someone who is meant to be your lover and best friend and feeling utterly alone. Many introverts have been in relationships where they felt unseen and overwhelmed, and they later spent years pushing love away so they would never again experience the loneliness of being with the wrong person. Have you ever done this? Are you doing it right now?

July 24

Reflection Questions

What is your favorite memory of a time when you were completely alone? Describe the scene. What did you see, smell, and taste? What were you doing, and how did it feel? What activities make you feel the greatest sense of fulfilment and connection? For me, it is having dinner parties, going for walks, having a cozy night in with my best friends, and expressing my creativity.

_____

_____

_____

_____

July 25

The Lonely Artist

"Writing is utter solitude, the descent into the cold abyss of oneself."

—Franz Kafka

No one is better acquainted with loneliness than the introverted artist. We have a kind of codependent relationship with loneliness. We need it in order to keep our most cherished companion, our art, by our side. While it's true that creativity blossoms in solitude, the question we must ask ourselves is: How much solitude? If you are struggling to reconcile your need for creative solitude with your desire for companionship, consider ways that you can fit both into your life. Perhaps this means going into your creative cave for a stretch to finish a project and then returning to a more "balanced" way of living and socializing afterwards.

July 26

Selfish or Indecisive?

All I want is to have my space,
to be blissfully alone,
and enjoy the sanctity of a solitude
that never makes any demands of me.
And then, after a while, I regret pushing people away.
All I want is to be touched,
to be joined at the heart with another person,
and enjoy the comfort of a true friend
who only asks that I be myself and allow her to do the same.
Am I the most selfish person in the world,
or simply indecisive?

July 27

FINDING YOUR PEOPLE

When you feel like you don't belong anywhere, loneliness becomes your home. But what if there were a place you could go to always feel welcomed and understood? I have discovered that there is no place more welcoming than a gathering of people who know what it means to not belong. That is why I love spoken word poetry slams so much.

Spoken word poetry gives a voice to those who feel unheard and misunderstood. Fringe dwellers, loners, people who identify as LGBTQ, people who don't identify as anything at all, people who were bullied and cast aside—these are my people. Not because we are so alike, but because we are each so different from everyone else that our strangeness bonds us. We instantly understand one another because we know how it feels to be the lonely puzzle piece that doesn't fit in. If you feel like you don't belong anywhere, look for the people who feel the same way; they have been searching for you, too.

July 28

SOLITUDE CHALLENGE

This month's challenge is simple, and I think you'll enjoy it. Find a way to make your solitude sweeter. Something as simple as updating your playlist and filling your home with music will work. You might also pull out a forgotten creative project or buy some new books and an extra-soft blanket.

July 29

Protectors of Solitude

While the right people will help alleviate our loneliness, the wrong ones will only aggravate it. Introverts need close friends who respect our need for solitude, while also enhancing it. Right now, you might be used to spending time with people who constantly pressure you to "come out of your shell." But it is possible to find friends who will protect, and even share, the sacred space of your solitude. Embracing your introversion, instead of apologizing for it, will help you attract such people.

July 30

Loneliness at Night

When I am feeling lonely, I love to go for long walks in the cold darkness of night. The chill in the air caresses my skin and reminds me that I am alive. All of a sudden, the emptiness feels expansive instead of isolating. My loneliness becomes an endless black sky, and the holes in my soul are filled with stars.

July 31

July Celebration

Even when you're feeling lonely, you are making progress in life. You are learning, growing, and processing. Write down a recent accomplishment or experience you would like to celebrate. Remember that your celebration can be something small and simple, such as spending more time with family or finally decluttering your office.

August

REFLECTIONS ON LOVE

"Have you ever been in love? Horrible isn't it? It makes you so vulnerable. It opens your chest and it opens up your heart and it means that someone can get inside you and mess you up."

—Neil Gaiman, *The Kindly Ones*

August 1

WHY YOU PUSH LOVE AWAY

Sometimes, introverts treat love, in all its forms, like an uninvited guest. We fear that it will sneak up on us at the wrong time. It will find us naked and exposed, looking like yesterday's leftovers and feeling totally unprepared for company. "Wait just a minute," we say. "Let me get dressed and comb my hair, and while I'm at it, I should really get another certificate, become a better conversationalist, and learn to control my emotions." So love gets impatient and looks for someone who is ready today. And that is what we had been fearing all along—that love would abandon us, leaving us to flail in the darkness of our own unfulfilled longing. It doesn't have to be this way. We let love into our messy heart in much the same way that we allow a dear friend to enter our untidy home. If it is a true friendship, we don't even apologize for the mess. We find a seat amid the chaos and accept that we are two flawed beings in an imperfect home.

This month's entries will help you to let in more love in your own introverted way.

August 2

BEING INTIMATE WITH YOURSELF

Introverts are pretty good at being intimate with ourselves. This is a step in the right direction, because being aware of who we are and what we believe prepares us for intimacy with others. Build on your relationship with you today by adding some romance to your solitude. Eat dinner by candlelight, set the mood with music, and spend some quality time alone with your own imagination.

August 3

Love between Two Introverts

People often ask me whether it is better for introverts to date a fellow introvert or an extrovert. Both pairings can work, but I have to admit, there is something special about love between two introverts. An introvert-introvert relationship provides a refreshing oasis in an increasingly loud world. It is a love formed on mutual acceptance with little need for compromise. It is a partnership with fewer words, but greater understanding. Together, you create a safe place where both of you have enough space to blossom.

August 4

August Book Nook

1. *Attached: The New Science of Adult Attachment and How It Can Help You Find—and Keep—Love* by Amir Levine and Rachel Heller
2. *Zen and the Art of Falling in Love* by Brenda Shoshanna
3. *Introverts in Love: The Quiet Way to Happily Ever After* by Sophia Dembling
4. *Quirkyalone: A Manifesto for Uncompromising Romantics* by Sasha Cagen
5. *Radical Honesty: How to Transform Your Life by Telling the Truth* by Brad Blanton

August 5

SMOOTHING THE SHARP EDGES

Do you sometimes fear that you'll never find your perfect match? You feel so different from everyone else that you wonder how you will find a partner who is a fit. Many of the people I have loved most in my life, both platonically and romantically, did not immediately pique my interest. They seemed like a mismatch, all elbows and knees to my gentle curves. But over the years, we learned to walk together despite our differences. When love finally arrived, it smoothed every sharp edge until the person felt like home. As you search for love, remember that time and understanding can shape the unlikeliest person into your perfect match.

August 6

THE QUIRKYALONE INTROVERT

"Quirkyalone is not anti-love. It is pro-love. It is not anti-dating. It is anti-compulsory dating. We tend to be romantics. We prefer to be single rather than settle."
—Sasha Cagen, www.quirkyalone.net

If you've been single for a long time and don't know why, you might be what author and coach Sasha Cagen calls "quirkyalone." Cagen describes quirkyalones as "uncompromising romantics" who would rather stay single than settle. She stresses that quirkyalone does not mean anti-love or anti-dating. You are simply embracing a love affair with your authentic self. If the right person arrives, you will welcome them with open arms. If not, you know how to be happy alone.

August 7

ACCEPTING LOVE IN ALL ITS FORMS

I love you. Many of us spend our whole lives longing to hear those three words. It's not enough to hear it from a parent, sibling, or friend. We want to hear it within the context of a romantic relationship. While it's true that romantic love is special, it is not meant to outshine every other form of love. We shouldn't ignore the I-love-you's from our dearest family and friends as we strive and strain to hear them from a lover. Remember that all forms of love are gifts that deserve our appreciation.

August 8

REFLECTION QUESTIONS

Have most of your past relationships been with introverts or extroverts? Which type do you prefer to be with, and why?

Are you happy with your current relationship status? If not, what do you want instead?

_____

_____

_____

_____

_____

_____

August 9
Setting Boundaries

One of the biggest mistakes introverts make in relationships is waiting too long to talk about boundaries. When you finally do express your needs, the other person feels confused and hurt. They can't understand why you suddenly need space when a couple of weeks ago you spent every waking moment together. Prevent future confusion by setting boundaries early on in the relationship. Let your love interest know that you will need time to yourself. Be sure to emphasize that your need for space doesn't mean you are unhappy in the relationship.

August 10
I See You

Have you ever noticed how intimate it feels to simply look a person in the eye? Holding another person's gaze is unnerving. It makes you feel naked and vulnerable, which also means that it makes you feel seen. Start looking people in the eye more often. If you have a partner, try setting a timer and staring into each other's eyes for five minutes. Most importantly, practice looking yourself in the eye. Stand in the mirror, hold your head high, and say, "I see you." This is what it looks like to stop hiding from yourself.

August 11
Spread the Love

If you're anything like me, you feel really excited when you stumble upon that rare unicorn of a person whom you can spend lots of time with without feeling drained. When you find such a friend, or lover, you might be tempted to focus all of your attention on them. It's important to remember that no one person can fulfill all your emotional needs. Be sure to schedule in time for yourself and the other people in your life so you don't completely smother your favorite playmate.

August 12
August Fortune Cookie

Let the fortune cookie decide your fate. Roll the dice, and read the fortune that coincides with the number you land on.

1. Congratulations! You are on your way to a new adventure.
2. A stranger will offer you an opportunity you can't resist.
3. Your love life will take a surprising turn in the coming days.
4. Your patience will be rewarded with a new opportunity at work.
5. Your dreams are worth the effort. Don't give up!
6. A secret admirer is preparing to make a move.
7. You will soon travel abroad for business and pleasure.

August 13

Watering Your Relationships

I am a terrible gardener. The only way I remember to water plants is when I see them dying. I can be just as bad at tending my relationships. I get so involved with whatever project I'm working on or internal crisis I'm untangling that I forget to keep in touch with the people I love. I've discovered that the best way to prevent both my plants and relationships from dying is to put them someplace where I can see them. Placing photos of my family and friends on my fridge and computer desktop reminds me to reach out. Putting little reminders in my calendar also helps: "Text Mom," "Send thank you note," "Call to say happy birthday."

August 14

Introvert Foreplay

You are a soft body
of hard-to-swallow contradictions,
strangely beautiful
and perfectly flawed.
Never change.

Peeling back the layers of one's personality is a form of foreplay; the slow, tender undressing of the soul is the definition of seduction. Many people can't get beyond the first layer. They're so busy fumbling with your overcoat that they never discover the French lace underneath. This is their loss, not yours.

August 15

Secret Fears That Repel Love

As introverts, we secretly fear losing ourselves in a relationship. We worry that we'll be totally engulfed by the other's needs, and we won't have anything left for ourselves. Our fears might drive us to subconsciously choose to be single, even though we say we want a relationship. If you're tired of coming home to an empty bed, and yet you still keep pushing good men or women away, consider the hidden fears at play. Ask yourself if you're truly willing to make space in your life for another person's needs and feelings.

August 16

Reflection Questions

Have you ever been with someone who made you feel truly seen? What did they see in you that others missed?
Is there a way that you could allow others to see this aspect of you more easily?

_____

_____

_____

_____

_____

_____

August 17

Rushed Intimacy

Have you ever felt too much pressure too soon in a relationship? Worst of all, perhaps the person you were dating made you feel guilty for not opening up right away. It's okay to want to take relationships at a slower pace. Introverts need to feel like the person we're with will give us the space and time we need to process our feelings. When someone tries to force intimacy, both emotional and physical, too quickly, they risk pushing us away. Paradoxically, we can fall in love much faster when a lover is patient, allowing us to open up in our own due time.

August 18

The Seduction of Authenticity

I am not like other women. I don't fall for the facade, the empty promises dressed in expensive suits. For me, honesty is a form of seduction. I like real people with real emotions who talk about real things. Let's skip the pretending and the efforts to impress. We'll dive straight into the center of a conversation and make the world disappear.

August 19

Single Together

I want to be single together.

I want to sit in tandem silence and know without a shadow of a doubt that it is not awkward.

I want to walk, and read, and dream together, building worlds without words.

I want to know that needing space is okay. That we will return to each other better than when we left.

I want to be alone in the same room as you.

I want to find solitude in your presence.

I want to be single with you.

August 20

Monthly Gratitude Moment

Even if you are single, there is love in your life. Make a long beautiful list of the people, animals, and experiences that light up your heart with love. Alternatively, you can focus on one love source and write in-depth about your appreciation and adoration for him, her, or it.

August 21

The Shoulds of Singlehood

Whether you are happy being single or you yearn for a relationship, you have likely felt like you are not where you *should* be. If you are content being single, you worry that you should want a relationship. If you do desperately want a relationship, you fear that your wanting will jinx your chances of finding love. You think you should just stop caring, and only then will your soulmate show up at your door. No matter what camp you fall into, I invite you to let go of the shoulds of being single. Be where you are and want what you want without questioning the validity of your desires. You have the right to be filled or unfulfilled in whatever manner you please.

August 22

This is How an Introvert Falls in Love

We introverts might be complicated souls, but our needs are simple, especially when it comes to love:

- We need your loyalty. Will you stick by us, keep our secrets, and cherish our friendship? If so, we will be fiercely loyal to you in return.
- We need your patience. Will you let us open slowly and relish in the slow bloom of our love? If so, we will let you into our secret world.
- We need your understanding. Will you notice the little things that we do and say that others miss? If so, we will forgive all your flaws.
- We need your honesty. Will you drop the facade and tell the truth about who you are and what you want? If so, we will make you our moon.

August 23

Learning to Let Love In

You've probably heard the saying, "Misery loves company." For introverts, the opposite is true. When we face hard times, we are more likely to push people away than to try to bring them down with us. Our misery loves to be alone. This is unfortunate because when we are at our lowest point, we become vulnerable and actually let our guard down for once. Our sadness can be fertile grounds for true connection to take root. The next time you are struggling, try something different. Reach out to someone who will listen without judgment and who won't try to fix you.

August 24

Reflection Questions

When you are in a relationship, what do you need from your partner in order to feel safe to open up and fall in love?

What would be the ideal timeline for physical intimacy for you? Are you honoring your needs, or do you feel pressure to be intimate sooner than you wish?

_____

_____

_____

_____

August 25

Letting Go After a Breakup

It's hard to let go after heartbreak. Breakups are especially tough for introverts because we must let go of the dream we had for the relationship. Our vibrant imagination makes for very colorful fantasies. The person we're grasping is long gone, but we're still trying to dream them back to life, like a balloon inflated by fantasies. Yes, it's difficult to let go, but doing so is an act of releasing ourselves. It is palms turned up and opened wide after being clenched for too long. It is freedom from misplaced hope followed by a long sigh of relief. So, go ahead and just release it all: the fantasies, the false hope, the safe haven that couldn't save you after all. Tape everything to a golden balloon. And let go.

August 26

Shallow Swimmers

Press an ear to my chest
and you'll hear the ocean.
Can you swim?
It's cold here
on the other side of the bed,
but I don't want to drown you.

Some people will never understand you. Your complexity stirs confusion, and even fear, in such people. They are shallow swimmers, easily drowned by the depths of your heart. They will try to change you. Don't give in. Resist the temptation to flatten your complexity and water down your soul. The moment you feel like you need to prove yourself in a relationship, it's time to begin looking for an exit. One of you will have to go.

August 27

The Heart Cannot Be Broken

The heart cannot be broken
but it can close like a rose
in reverse bloom,
A closed heart still beats
though it's forgotten what it's beating for,
And an open heart still hurts
though it's decided not to hide.
The heart cannot be broken
but it can cry and bleed and die,
The heart cannot be broken
but it can go deaf to love
and forget to dance.
My heart cannot be broken
It can hurt and hide
and cry,
but it can also sing, love, feel, beat, dream, believe,
and keep me alive.

August 28

Love Challenge

This month's challenge is simple, but you might find it difficult. Say "I love you" to someone you don't normally say it to. Whether the person is a friend, family member, or lover, let him or her know how you feel. It doesn't have to be a grand declaration. You can casually slip an "I love you" into everyday conversation, tack it onto the end of a telephone call, write it in a text, or send it in an email. Just do it, dearest. It won't hurt nearly as much as you think it will.

August 29

The One Who Still Haunts Your Dreams

To me you are a cemetery
of sun-filled memories.
I mourn you in the day,
and revive you in my dreams.

In life there are people you think of often. You carry them in your heart like crayons in a box, allowing them to color all your fantasies. Just the thought of them makes your world brighter. And then there are people you would rather forget. Yet, your subconscious still clings to their memory. Even if you manage to avoid thinking of them when you are awake, they haunt your dreams.

- Who are the people you still wonder about? You think, *whatever happened to so-and-so?*
- Who do you think of when you see the most beautiful sunrise and remember that you are alive?
- Who is it that still clings to the depths of your subconscious, no matter how many times you try to let go?
- Who do you hope is thinking of you right now?
- Who probably thinks of you every day?

August 30
Slow Bloom Love

I have always preferred when love sneaks up on me. I'm like a deer that you have to approach slowly, preferably with food in your hand, lest I bound off in fear. If you sit in my general vicinity for a few weeks, months, or even years, not asking anything of me, I'll lose the urge to run from you and might actually invite you to come closer. In this day and age of instant gratification, of swiping and tapping our way to love, it's hard to have a slow-blooming relationship. Often, these kinds of drawn-out courtships happen by "coincidence," which is really just the skeptic's word for magic. If it feels like love is taking its sweet time finding you, maybe it already has, and it is just approaching you slowly, carrot in hand, trying its best not to scare you off.

August 31
August Celebration

What is your celebration for this month? No matter how small and insignificant they may seem, your triumphs deserve to be acknowledged. Celebrate every bit of progress. Write your celebration in your journal, tell a friend, and give yourself a little reward, if you like.

September

COZY CORNERS

"The ache for home lives in all of us. The safe place where we can go as we are and not be questioned."
—Maya Angelou, *All God's Children Need Traveling Shoes*

September 1
An Introvert's Dwelling

Is there a place you can go and just be yourself—a sacred space that offers solitude and sanctuary from the demands of the outside world? For introverts, especially, it is important to have such a place. The world and all its chaos exhausts us. We need a place where we can slow down, process our experiences, reflect, and just be.

Even though having a comfortable home is essential to our well-being, it can at times feel out of reach. For introverts, the sheer effort of building a life leaves little energy to build a home—let alone a home that reflects our unique values and style.

For a long time, I lived in furnished homes. This allowed me to live light and feel free, unburdened by the weight of possessions and the stress of building a home of my own. Nowadays, it is becoming more and more important to me that my physical space reflects who I am. I want my home to be an outward expression of my inner world: my appreciation for beauty and art, my strong creative streak, my sensitivity, my love of simplicity. I want to be surrounded by colors, textures, and fragrances that inspire me. It's important for your home to reflect your values and needs, as well. This month's entries will help you to create a home, and a life, that brings you all the quiet comforts your heart desires.

September 2
WHAT DOES HOME MEAN TO YOU?

For most of us, the word *home* conjures many memories of family and traditions. We recall the familiar aroma of our favorite home-cooked meals. We hear the sound of parents and siblings laughing, arguing, or lecturing. And sometimes, the word reminds us of disappointments and regrets. No matter what home means to you, its meaning is forever etched in your very being. What memories arise when you hear the word *home*? List the words, sensations, and experiences that come to mind.

September 3
THE NEED FOR A HOME BASE

Many introverts desperately crave the stability that a home can offer. We need an anchor to keep us in place as the world shifts madly beneath our feet. If you're like me and your childhood was marked by divorce and frequent moving, you want your home to be a sanctuary—a place you can count on no matter what tremors shake your world. Or maybe your turbulent childhood has made your pendulum swing in the opposite direction, and you continue to move from place to place as you did in your youth. Regardless of whether you choose a gypsy lifestyle like I once did or you are more rooted, it's important to have some kind of home base, a place you can go and always feel safe. Do you have such a place?

September 4
September Book Nook

Here is a list of books to help you create a more peaceful and inviting living space:

1. *The Joy of Less, A Minimalist Living Guide: How to Declutter, Organize, and Simplify Your Life* by Francine Jay
2. *The Cozy Life: Rediscover the Joy of the Simple Things Through the Danish Concept of Hygge* by Pia Edberg
3. *The Nesting Place: It Doesn't Have to Be Perfect to Be Beautiful* by Myquillyn Smith
4. *The Bee Cottage Story: How I Made a Muddle of Things and Decorated My Way Back to Happiness* by Frances Schultz, Newell Turner, and Trevor Tondro
5. *The Life-Changing Magic of Tidying Up: The Japanese Art of Decluttering and Organizing* by Marie Kondo

September 5

The Beauty of Minimalism

There is a zen teaching that says in order to make a space more beautiful, one must remove unnecessary objects. As an introvert, you might find this minimalistic approach especially appealing. After all, a chaotic environment leads to a chaotic mind, and your mental landscapes are cluttered enough as it is.

Strive to only surround yourself with objects that either have a definite purpose or bring you joy. A beautiful painting is useful because its colors light up your heart. A coffee table has a purpose because it provides a surface for your tea or a book. Your 1980s prom dress, on the other hand, brings no real purpose or pleasure to your daily life.

September 6

Letting Go of Excess

It can be hard to let go of objects you've lived with for a long time, even if you feel overwhelmed by clutter. I'm reminded of those reality shows about hoarders, who filled every inch of their living space with junk they couldn't bring themselves to part with. I noticed that, in many cases, the hoarding was triggered by the loss of a relationship or a loved one. While hoarders believe that holding onto objects will protect them from more loss, really, the opposite is true. Letting go of the clutter in your life will create space for new gifts to flow in. Make a plan to let go of the excess in your home so that you can free up precious real estate in your mind and heart.

September 7

Revealing the Invisible Beauty

Sometimes, it's difficult to let go of objects because it means we will have to sit alone with ourselves without distractions. In our mind, having more physical objects equals less space for our secret insecurities, which leads to a false sense of comfort. But our possessions often get in the way of the invisible elements that truly make a home glow: love, laughter, music, and joy. Even if it's scary, make an effort to let go of what you no longer need so you can reveal the beauty that has been hiding in plain sight all along.

September 8

Reflection Questions

What objects can you let go of today to create more peace and simplicity in your home?

How can you add more invisible beauty to your home? In other words, how can you add more laughter, love, music, and joy to your space?

_____

_____

_____

_____

_____

_____

September 9
Building Together

One of the main reasons introverts avoid organizing and decorating our home is because we find the process overwhelming. All the shopping, decision making, arranging, and rearranging can be absolutely exhausting. But creating a beautiful living space doesn't have to be stressful. When I moved into my current home, I decided to enlist the help of one of my best friends.

He accompanied me on my shopping trip and helped deliver the final verdict when I was indecisive. He also assisted with the assembling of furniture and hanging pictures. The activities that once felt daunting became fun. I discovered that building a home doesn't have to be a solitary effort even if you live alone.

September 10
Uncomfortable Living Situations

Have you ever lived in a home that you just didn't feel comfortable in? It can be painful for introverts when our home is not our own. We find ourselves inhabiting a space that is too cramped, cluttered, and chaotic.

What do you do when you find yourself in a living situation that is less than ideal? I recommend following the advice of Theodore Roosevelt, who said, "Do what you can, with what you have, where you are."

If you imagine yourself living by the ocean, put a painting of the sea in your bedroom. If you want a garden, get some potted plants and nurture them as you would an enchanted garden. One day, your home will blossom into the oasis you envisioned.

September 11
A Bedtime Oasis

For introverts, our bedroom is so much more than just sleeping quarters. It is where we read, dream, and reflect. When we climb into our bed at night, it becomes our fortress, protecting us from the cares of the day. In the morning, we love to linger in the comforting embrace of our blanket cocoon. Here are some ideas to make your bedroom an oasis of solitude:

- Decorate it in relaxing shades of blue and white.
- Infuse the air with the scent of calming essential oils.
- Clear away all the clutter on your dresser and display only your favorite books and treasures.
- Before you get ready for bed, turn down the corner of your duvet, set out a good book, and prop your pillows up to welcome you after you finish your nighttime routine.

September 12
September Fortune Cookie

Let the fortune cookie decide your fate. Roll the dice, and read the fortune that coincides with the number you land on.

1. Your talents will capture the attention of someone important.
2. People are attracted to your calm nature.
3. Others find it difficult to resist your beautiful hands.
4. Self-discovery is a lifelong process.
5. Pennies from heaven will find their way to your doorstep this year!
6. Look for the lesson in every problem.

September 13
Reviving Your Living Room

Have you ever had a living room that lacked life? The living room is meant to be the heartbeat of a home. It is where you go to relax with a good book or have lazy conversations with family members and best friends. But sometimes a living room is not up to snuff. Everything about the space is cold and uninviting, from the uncomfortable couch and the bare floors to the colorless walls and cluttered corners—the room simply feels un-liveable.

For an introvert like me, a living room is a place to work, create, relax, and play. It needs to be both comfortable and functional, and it has to feel like a sanctuary. If your living room lacks life, remember that it's not frivolous to invest energy into reviving it. A beautiful living room will rejuvenate and inspire you.

September 14
Finding Nourishment

If the living room is the heart of a home, the kitchen is its belly—not just because it's where we go to eat, but also because it is the hub of creation. Our kitchen is the womb in which lively discussions and vibrant meals are born. It is a place of comfort and nourishment, or at least it can be. If you're anything like me, you associate food with love, and that can be a dangerous combination if you're not feeding or loving yourself properly. Keep your kitchen clean and well-stocked with food so that you always feel nourished and cared for.

September 15
Freshening Up

The bathroom is, among other things, where we go to rinse away the day's worries and feel renewed. If you have children, the bathroom might also be the only place where you can have some privacy. Don't underestimate the value of this small room. If you have a bathtub, keep it shiny so you can indulge in a restorative soak when you need to. Clean the mirror so you don't have to wake up to grime and soap scum each day. It's nice to be able to look at yourself—all fresh and clean—without two week's worth of toothpaste splatter getting in the way. I also like to keep essential oils and peppermint hand soap on hand to create a spa-like atmosphere.

September 16
Reflection Questions

What would your dream home be like? What small changes can you make to your home today to get closer to that vision? How can you make your living room more alive and inviting?

_____

_____

_____

_____

_____

_____

September 17
HIDDEN CHAOS

What are you hiding in your closet? More accurately, what is your closet allowing you to hide from? Maybe it holds keepsakes you know you should no longer keep, such as presents from exes. You might also be a book or DVD hoarder. Maybe you even have a collection of VHS videos stored in there. As easy as it may seem to shove these items in the closet and forget about them, the truth is they are still taking up space in the periphery of both your home and your mind. Don't wait until you move house to go through the abyss of unwanted objects. Grab a big garbage bag and tell yourself you're just going to have a quick look through things, and see what happens.

September 18
HOME WORK

You might not have an office in your home, but you probably have a space that you designate for work, such as your living room couch or a desk in your bedroom. Having your "office" in the same place where you sleep, play, or go online can confuse your brain and make it hard to concentrate. Shifting the atmosphere in a room before you set off to work helps. I like to put on some piano instrumentals or zen meditation music. This transforms my couch or kitchen table into a workspace and tells my brain that it's time to create. It's also important to be comfortable when you work. Your brain doesn't like being treated like a deprived slave.

September 19
ROMANTIC SPACES

Being an INFP personality type (introversion, intuition, feeling, and perception of the Myers-Briggs Type Indicator), I love beauty and romance, and nowhere is this more evident than in my home. I keep fresh roses in my kitchen and potted red flowers on my desk. I decorate the living room with velvet, fake fur, and metallic textiles and listen to jazz music as I cook fragrant meals.

Adding romance to your home brings magic to the everyday. Why not try it out for yourself? The next time you're at the grocery store, pick up some scented candles, a bouquet of flowers, and some fresh herbs and spices for cooking. You can also freshen up your music playlist with soulful tunes that awaken the heart of your home.

September 20
MONTHLY GRATITUDE MOMENT

What aspects of your living space are you most grateful for? If you're finding it difficult to come up with things you like about your current home, think back to past homes and write down what you appreciated about them.

September 21
Outdoor Living

"Nature is not a place to visit. It is home."
—Gary Snyder, *The Practice of the Wild*

The great outdoors provides a natural sanctuary for introverts. It is a place where we can go to breathe deeply, escape our worries, and refresh our soul. Best of all, it's free. You don't have to pay or plan for it. Just walk outside, find a quiet patch of green, and enjoy the rejuvenating benefits of being in nature.

Here are some easy ways to enjoy the outdoors:

- go for a walk, run, or hike
- swim in a nearby lake or river
- lie on the grass and watch the clouds pass
- sit under a shady tree and read a book
- do yoga in the park
- do stand-up paddle boarding
- go skating, snowshoeing, or cross-country skiing

September 22

At Home Inside Your Head

Many introverts feel most at home inside our own head. We love to wander the deep forests of our imagination. Often, we retreat to our imaginary world to escape a harsh reality. In the real world, we may never feel understood or fully accepted; but in our fantasies, we find a safe and welcoming space where we are free to be as weird as we like. To make your mind even more inviting, try "decorating" your mental landscapes with positive self-talk.

- Refer to yourself in the third person as "honey," "sweetie," "darling," or "my love."
- Give your mind treats to look forward to. For example, if you have to do tedious mental work for a while, reward yourself with a nap or movie.
- Listen to uplifting music, zen mantras, or subliminal message audios.
- Read affirmations before bed or upon waking, when your subconscious is most impressionable.

September 23

When Home is a Human Being

Sometimes, home is a person. It is a lover, parent, or lifelong friend. Even for independent introverts—perhaps, *especially*, for independent introverts—having a "home base" relationship is essential. We need a special friend who opens their door and makes space for us in every area of their life. Do you have such a friend? More importantly, are you willing to *be* that type of friend?

September 24
REFLECTION QUESTIONS

How can you add more romance to your home this week?
What makes a person feel like home to you?

_____

_____

_____

_____

_____

_____

_____

September 25
FILLING THE SPACE

Have you ever felt like you had to contain and restrict your true essence? You might not have been doing this consciously. Somewhere along the line, you let the bigger, bolder characters fill the space with their energy. The same thing can happen in your home. You might let your partner or roommate dictate the tone and style of your space while you just go with the flow.

It's important for your home to be a reflection of you, even if only in one room. And if you don't have a whole room to yourself, at the very least have a cozy corner that reflects your unique personality, values, and tastes.

September 26
Objects You've Outgrown

"If one changes internally, one should not continue to live with the same objects."
—Anaïs Nin, *The Diary of Anaïs Nin, Vol. 4: 1944–1947*

Have you outgrown the objects in your home? Perhaps the artwork and decorations reflect a phase of life that you thought you had left behind. It's hard to fully embrace a new stage of life when your home is a constant reminder of who you were five years ago. Getting rid of clothes that don't fit anymore and shedding decorations and furniture that you've outgrown is a way of moving on. It says, "I know that this life doesn't fit me anymore, and it never will again." You don't necessarily have to replace everything right away. Leave a wall empty until you come across a painting that sings to you—not the student you, or the newly married you—but the you that exists in the here and now.

September 27
Living with Roommates

Living with roommates can be pure torture for introverts, especially if your flatmate likes to make small talk with you early in the morning or have lots of parties. Aside from hiding in your room all the time, another way to deal with roommate problems is to actually let them know when something is not working. I know this is difficult, but it's necessary, as silent resentments will quickly poison the atmosphere of a home. There are plenty of ways to get things off your chest. You can set up a roommate meeting or just blurt it out as you pass each other in the kitchen. You can also write a text, email, or note—just be sure to keep the tone friendly as angry messages can be more damaging than arguing face-to-face.

September 28
Cozy Corner Challenge

Choose a part of your home to makeover or makeunder. Here are some ideas:

- Declutter and organize your desk
- Make your couch more inviting with soft and beautiful textiles
- Use organizer baskets to make your living room more orderly
- Change the mood of a room with lower or higher wattage light bulbs
- Give your bathroom the spa treatment with plush towels, essential oils, and artisan soaps

September 29
Inviting Others In

Introverts are often just as protective of our home interiors as we are of our mental landscapes. We don't open it up to just anyone. But even introverts can appreciate the way the right guests can light up a home. In fact, many introverts love hosting gatherings because it gives us more control. We get to decide who to invite and how long the get-together will last. I have always liked hosting dinner parties because I enjoy cooking and creating a beautiful atmosphere. It is also my way of showing my friends and family that I love them. If you're not used to having guests, I recommend that you keep the gathering small and the timeframe short. Even if you enjoy hosting, it can deplete your precious energy quite quickly.

September 30
SEPTEMBER CELEBRATION

September is a time of year when everything feels fresh and new. It's a great time to celebrate your victories, no matter how small. Write down any bit of progress that you are proud of today.

October

Introvert Unmasked

"We live our deepest soul's desires not by intending to change who we are, but by intending to be who we are."
—Oriah Mountain Dreamer, *The Dance*

October 1

TIRED OF PRETENDING

"The most exhausting thing in life is being insincere."
—Anne Morrow Lindbergh, *Gift from the Sea*

We all wear masks, but few of us realize the toll it takes on us. Some might say that the world is a stage anyway, so why not play the part that helps you to fit in? If you've ever performed on stage you know that becoming someone else, even for just a few moments, is hard work. It takes a lot of practice and memorization, and the performance itself is exhausting. Actors get to relax back into their true personality when they walk off stage, but what about you?

When do you get to shed the mask and just be yourself? If you've been feeling weary and don't know why, it might be because your body and mind are tired of pretending. You are secretly feeling what bestselling author Elizabeth Gilbert described when she fell in love and began a same-sex relationship with her best friend, Rayya Elias, and then decided to go public about it. She explained: "Pretending is demeaning, and it makes you weak and confused, and it's also a lot of work. I don't do that kind of work anymore." You might not have realized that quitting was an option—that you could resign from the tedious work of pretending, turn in your cumbersome uniform, and just be you again. It absolutely is.

Right now, you are likely in the habit of adjusting your preferences to suit your audience. You are a great actor, playing to the crowd. But living authentically often means being a bad actor. You care more about what you think of yourself than what others think of you.

This month's entries will give you permission to stop pretending and to finally relax into your true personality. As you make your way through each day, remember that it took a long time to master the different roles that you play. Don't be discouraged if you can't flick a switch and "be yourself" overnight. Be patient and kind to yourself. The true you is worth the wait.

October 2

MEETING YOURSELF

Going through life wearing a mask is a lot like living with a stranger. You don't really know anything about the person sitting beside you. Sure, you know the basics, like what kind of food they like and their daily routines. But when it comes to the bigger questions, such as their true values, beliefs, gifts, and dreams, you are stumped. You can become acquainted with your true self by asking yourself some simple questions:

- What do I know to be true?
- What do I no longer believe?
- What is unique or unusual about me?
- What should I have learned by now?
- What makes me angry?
- What makes me cry?
- What makes me laugh?

October 3

Facing the Truth

The mask is nothing more than a pretty lie. That's why the truth is so revealing. At every point in my journey toward a more authentic life, I had to face uncomfortable truths. Before I got divorced, I had to face the truth that I got married for the wrong reasons and I was not happy. Before I set out on my hero's journey to find purpose, I had to face the truth that I couldn't force myself to live a status quo life; I had to make my own path. No matter how scary the truth may seem, it is worth exploring because a life built on lies may look good on the outside, but it always feels hollow on the inside.

October 4

October Book Nook

1. *Introvert Power: Why Your Inner Life Is Your Hidden Strength* by Laurie Helgoe
2. *I Know I'm in There Somewhere: A Woman's Guide to Finding Her Inner Voice and Living a Life of Authenticity* by Helene Brenner
3. *The Mask of Masculinity: How Men Can Embrace Vulnerability, Create Strong Relationships, and Live Their Fullest Lives* by Lewis Howes
4. *The Secret Lives of Introverts: Inside Our Hidden World* by Jenn Granneman
5. *1 Page at a Time: A Daily Creative Companion* by Adam J. Kurtz

October 5

The Pain of Unmasking

"We all wear masks, and the time comes when we cannot remove them without removing some of our own skin."
—Andre Berthiaume, *Contretemps: Nouvelles*

How much skin have you put into your mask? Do you feel like your relationships, career, and friendships hinge on you keeping up the facade? I don't blame you. A mask is a form of armor that shields you from rejection—or so it seems. Often, your armor causes you more pain than you realize. It's important to ask yourself, does the risk of removing the mask outweigh the pain of never being seen?

October 6

Revealing Your Blue Skin

Many introverts wear masks to hide our strangeness. The problem with hiding our unusual quirks and preferences is that it prevents our tribe from finding us. In the poem "Masks," Shel Silverstein wrote about two people with hidden blue skin and how their efforts to hide their true colors made it impossible for them to spot each other. There are others who feel just as strange and alone as you do. They have tried desperately to locate you, but when they look up, all they find is a sea of carefully constructed masks. Make it easier for the right people to find you by revealing your "blue skin." Even just a sliver will do for now. Share more of your opinions, pet peeves, and obsessions, even if they seem a bit weird. Wear clothes and jewelry that tell others who you really are. It probably won't be as scary as you think; revealing your true self can be fun.

October 7

FOLLOWING YOUR CURIOSITIES

Often, revealing our true selves is a matter of following rather than finding. We follow our little obsessions and curiosities until they lead us to something bigger, like, say, our life's purpose or our soul tribe. When we land on lush ground, we use it as a launchpad to aim for the stars and discover our inner moonlight.

October 8

REFLECTION QUESTIONS

What is the difficult truth about your life that you've been avoiding?

What is your "blue skin"? In other words, what are the unusual qualities that you've been hiding from the world?

_____

_____

_____

_____

_____

_____

_____

_____

_____

_____

October 9

Preventing Yourself from Feeling Overwhelmed

We introverts tend to sabotage big changes because we overthink things and get overwhelmed. Luckily, shedding your mask and revealing more of your true self doesn't have to be overwhelming.

You can do so gradually in your own quiet way. The question I often ask my coaching clients is, "What is one thing you can do in the next three months that will get you closer to your goal?" If your goal is to be more authentic, your one thing might be revisiting a childhood passion or exploring a new form of creative expression.

October 10

Letting Go of Past Personas

Have you ever reconnected with a distant relative who still thinks of you as a child? This well-intentioned auntie or uncle assumes that you are still the sweet, shy little kid you were when you were twelve years old. And, sure, some remnants of that child version of yourself may remain, but you are all grown up now. As your limbs grew, so, too, did the many layers of your personality. You might feel tempted to slip back into a past persona to please people like your relatives who don't seem ready for the real you yet. Don't give in. Let go of past versions of yourself so you can fully embrace who you are today.

October 11

Friendships that No Longer Fit

The right people will make it easier for you to be yourself. Even friends who are surprised by the changes you're undergoing will make an effort to get reacquainted with the you they never knew. Some friendships, however, simply won't fit anymore. This can be painful and will most likely make you feel guilty. Perhaps, you'll even feel tempted to go back to pretending to keep the friendship alive. A better option is to focus on the people who embrace the more authentic version of you and let the ill-fitting friendships naturally fall away.

October 12

October Fortune Cookie

Let the fortune cookie decide your fate. Roll the dice, and read the fortune that coincides with the number you land on.

1. Now is the time to try something new.
2. Tragic endings mark a beautiful new beginning.
3. Time and nature heal all wounds.
4. You will live a long and peaceful life.
5. Help! I'm being held captive in a Chinese bakery!
6. You will see an old friend in a new light today.

HOLDING YOUR GROUND

It takes courage to be yourself, but the right people will respect your resolve to stay true to your convictions. Be inspired by the story of Diego Rivera and Frida Kahlo's first encounter. A young Kahlo was watching Diego paint when his jealous wife, Lupe, began to insult her relentlessly.

As Diego Rivera would later recount in his book *My Art, My Life: An Autobiography,* Kahlo held her ground, returning Lupe's icy stare. Kahlo's unwavering resolve so thoroughly disarmed Diego's jealous wife that her anger was transformed into admiration. "Look at that girl! Small as she is," she said, "she does not fear a tall, strong woman like me. I really like her." Remember Kahlo's quiet courage the next time you are tempted to hide your power. Sometimes, staying true to yourself is as simple as standing in place and looking someone in the eye.

October 14

Feeling Proud

It's easier to be yourself when you recognize that there is no shame in being an introvert. A while ago, I made an inspirational video called "Proud to be an Introvert," which I have transcribed below. I hope the words inspire you to wear your true personality with pride.

Proud to be an Introvert

When you're an introvert living in an extrovert's world, you spend a lot of time feeling misunderstood. People wonder . . .

Why are you so quiet? Why do you keep wandering off? Why would you want to be alone when there are parties to go to, people to meet, and adventures to be had?

They don't understand that for an introvert, our adventures begin on the inside. Our imagination gives us wings, carrying us to new worlds. We are the thinkers, the creators, the dreamers. We may be still and silent, but we are soaring.

So when you look at us sitting alone or daydreaming or wandering off by ourselves, don't feel sorry for us. We may be quiet, but don't underestimate our power. We know more than we say, we think more than we speak, and we observe more than you know.

We're introverts, and that doesn't make us "failed extroverts." We grew up thinking there was something wrong with us, but the truth is that introverts are so much more than what meets the eye.

We are deep divers in a world of shallow swimmers. We know how to listen, not just to words but also to the subtle messages carried on the wings of silence. Give us the freedom to be who we were meant to be, and you'll see how much introverts have to offer the world.

It's true that some people might never understand us, and that's okay, because when you know how to stand alone, the crowd can't knock you down.

Please don't try to change us into extroverts. We don't want to wear a mask. We're introverts, and that's something to be proud of.

You can find the video on my YouTube channel: Michaela Chung.

October 15
EMBRACING THIS STAGE

Part of being your most authentic self is fully accepting whatever stage of life you're in right now. Embrace the mistakes and the messiness of your twenties. Welcome the solid ground and rootedness of your thirties. If you are in a single phase, enjoy the freedom. If you are married with young children, relish the sense of companionship and purpose. I haven't reached my forties yet, but I hope that when I do, I will still see possibility on the horizon. I will know that the past is not where I belong. The here and now is my home, and embracing this moment brings out the me I was meant to be.

October 16

REFLECTION QUESTIONS

What relationships no longer fit you?
How can you more fully embrace the stage of life you're in right now?

_____

_____

_____

October 17

REFLECTIONS

When you look in the mirror
who do you see,
do you see you
or do you see me?
Are you searching for you
in a face that's not yours,
looking for answers
on the sands of my shores?
Look in from the outside
and soon you will see,
I am not you
and you are not me.
We are two people
with one clumsy name,
both of us human
yet not quite the same.

October 18

Comparing and Despairing

We all fall prey to the green-eyed monster on occasion. For introverts, it is all too easy to compare ourselves to extroverts and feel pretty lousy for it. But when you look to others for your sense of self-worth, you don't realize that you are comparing their most sparkling qualities to your darkest insecurities. Remember that people who possess the qualities you lack aren't any better than you. They are just as flawed, but in different ways. The next time your mind tries to trick you into comparing and despairing, try to look at yourself from an outsider's perspective. Is it possible that someone is envious of *you*?

October 19

Focusing on Progress

The only person you should be comparing yourself to is you. You're not the same person you were ten years ago. And if you look around, you'll realize that the world has changed, too. What made you weird as a kid is now your greatest asset. One of my personal mottos is "progress over perfection." You're not perfect, but you're better than you were before, and that's what really matters.

October 20

MONTHLY GRATITUDE MOMENT

List at least five supposed flaws and five strengths that you are grateful for. If you like, choose one quality from each list and write more in-depth about why you are thankful for them.

October 21

LOOKING THROUGH THE WRONG LENS

Often, when you feel bad about yourself, it's because you are looking through the eyes of someone else. You let naysayers and trolls sneak into your life and distort how you see yourself. Take back your power by saying goodbye to people who make you feel less-than. If someone else's opinions about you are taking up too much of your headspace, clear the clutter by writing the naysayer a letter and letting your emotions pour out on the page. You don't have to send the letter. Tuck it away in a place you won't look for a while, or burn it. Do whatever feels the most freeing.

October 22

THE TRAP OF CARING TOO MUCH

The reason that many of us stray so far from our authentic selves is that we care too much about what others think. We let our parents, friends, classmates, and even people we've never met in real life dictate our destiny.

Take a moment to recall all of the things that you have done to impress, please, or gain acceptance from other people. Brace yourself—the list is probably pretty long. If you're like me, it will include some major life choices, such as where you went to school, what degree you chose, the jobs you pursued, the people you dated or didn't date, and the places you lived. Now imagine what choices you would have made if you loved and accepted yourself 100 percent.

October 23

PARENTING YOUR FEAR

The underlying force that keeps our mask intact is always fear. Fear that we are not loveable just as we are. Fear that we will fail. Fear that we are not enough. The secret to letting go of your fear and revealing your true self is to parent it. Sit with your fear, look her in the face, and comfort her. You can even tell her that she can hang around if she wants, but you're not going to entertain her.

October 24

Reflection Questions

If a person were to be jealous of you, what would they admire and desire most?

Take a moment to reflect on how you've grown in different areas of your life over the last five years. What life lessons have you learned? How have you matured? What challenges have you overcome?

_____

_____

_____

_____

_____

_____

October 25

Letting the Dark Dance with the Light

We love ourselves completely when we embrace the dark and the light, the good and the bad. Many of us only want to accept and share the "good" aspects of our personality. I prefer to live by the words of Carl Jung, who said, "I would rather be whole than good." How would it feel to stop trying so hard to be good and allow the dark to dance with the light? What might your shadows look like in the brightness of day?

October 26

QUALITY TIME

As an introvert, you might spend a lot of time alone with yourself, but is it quality time? In his book, *The Five Love Languages*, Gary D. Chapman explains that we each need to be loved in a language that we can understand. One of the five love languages he outlines is quality time. At first, I scoffed at this—*obviously everyone wants quality time with their partner.* I later realized that while most people want time with their significant other, they don't necessarily need *quality* time.

Your authentic self needs you to spend quality time with her, doing the things that make her feel happy and cared for. Delight her with fun little excursions, treat her to life's little pleasures, listen to her through meditation. Most important, love her by bringing her out from behind the mask and allowing her to roam free in all areas of your life.

October 27

JUST BEING

Our extrovert-biased culture worships constant busyness and productivity. But this way of life is exhausting for introverts. Not only that, it also makes us lose touch with our true self. Our authentic self is a confusion of blurred lines when we are constantly whirring about, trying our best to do as the extroverts do. Bring her back into focus by slowing down, sitting down, staying still, and just *being*.

October 28

AUTHENTICITY CHALLENGE

Remember when I asked you in the entry on October 9 what is the one thing you can do in the next three months to achieve your goal? Your challenge for this month is to put that one thing into practice. Remember, you don't have to make a drastic change. A single small action step can make a big difference.

October 29

WHAT DO YOU WANT?

This is a tough question for introverts to answer. Many of us have spent our whole lives suppressing our desires in order to fit in. Now that we actually have the option to "fit out" and shape our lives as we please, we feel tempted to run back to the mold. There is comfort in the certainty of a cookie-cutter existence. Resist the temptation to let others shape you. It's time to ask the difficult questions and open your arms wide enough to catch all the possibilities that a life of your own brings. So, let's try this again. *What do you want?*

October 30

Taking the Plunge

Shedding your mask and living authentically all begins with a decision to be sincere about who you are. Be honest about what you want, need, and feel. Get acquainted with your true opinions, preferences, likes, dislikes. And whenever you face the choice to lie about who you are and what you believe, choose to tell the truth instead. This will seem scary at first, but remember: sharing your authentic self with others is like learning to swim in the deep end. It gets easier with each stroke, and soon you start to enjoy the way your feet don't touch the bottom anymore. You are no longer a shallow swimmer, but rather a person of depth and substance, someone you actually want to wade through life with.

October 31

October Celebration

Write down your celebration for this month, no matter how small. You can celebrate a time when you wanted to quit but didn't, or when you were afraid to do something but did it anyway. Every bit of progress counts and is worth celebrating.

November

QUIET GRATITUDE

"Walk as if you are kissing the Earth with your feet."
—Thich Nhat Hanh, *Peace Is Every Step:*
The Path of Mindfulness in Everyday Life

November 1

Singing Your Own Praises

"Piglet noticed that even though he had a Very Small Heart, it could hold a rather large amount of Gratitude."
—A. A. Milne, *Winnie-the-Pooh*

As an introvert, you might have grown up feeling anything but grateful for your personality. You tried to cure your introversion by mimicking extroverted behavior. Of course, this didn't work because you can't fix what isn't broken. You are an introvert. You like people, but sometimes you like your alone time more. You think deeply and choose your words carefully. You enjoy different pastimes than the extrovert down the street. None of this makes you a bad person. In fact, there are billions of other people who share your preferences. So, let's try a different approach, shall we?

Let's try on a little self-acceptance for size. Instead of trying to fix or cure, let's celebrate our strengths. For the longest time, I saw my quietness as a fatal flaw, a sign that I was not friendly or feminine enough. Now, I see it as just another piece of the intricate mosaic that is my personality.

Alongside my quietness, there is also intuition, wisdom, and an ability to read between the lines. Sure, I speak slowly and pause often, but I am singing on the inside. Those who matter can hear my silent song. This month's entries will help you to see the beauty in your introverted nature and guide you toward singing your own praises (quietly, of course).

November 2
Sharing Your Treasures

As an introvert, you might feel strange about admitting your strengths and successes. You try not to talk yourself up in fear that you'll suffer the consequences. You imagine that people will think you're arrogant or they will be jealous and reject you. Perhaps, you worry that you'll "jinx" your good fortune by acknowledging it. After all, as a child you were told not to share your wishes or they wouldn't come true.

But there is merit in sharing your successes—not to brag, but to acknowledge how far you've come. Talking about your good fortune is a way of saying "thank you" and "more, please." So, go ahead and acknowledge the many treasures of your introversion, even if only in a whisper to yourself or in the pages of your journal.

If you're having trouble recognizing your introverted strengths, I've outlined some examples in the upcoming entries.

November 3
#1 You Observe and Understand

"You see things. You keep quiet about them. And you understand."
—Stephen Chbosky, *The Perks of Being a Wallflower*

Introverts are known for standing on the sidelines. We are the ones who hang out along the edges of the party, and for good reason. Fringe dwellers have the best view. From a distance we are able to see the world objectively. As we quietly observe our surroundings, we gain a deep understanding of things that others might not even notice. Be thankful for your observant nature because it helps you see the bigger picture, while you appreciate life's beautiful intricacies at the same time.

November 4

NOVEMBER BOOK NOOK

Here are some books to help you cultivate more gratitude for your introversion and your life.

1. *A Simple Act of Gratitude: How Learning to Say Thank You Changed My Life* by John Kralik
2. *Quiet: The Power of Introverts in a World That Can't Stop Talking* by Susan Cain
3. *Gratitude: A Way of Life* by Louise L. Hay
4. *The Empath's Survival Guide: Life Strategies for Sensitive People* by Judith Orloff
5. *Living Life as a Thank You: The Transformative Power of Daily Gratitude* by Nina Lesowitz and Mary Beth Sammons

November 5

#2 YOU DON'T GET LOST IN THE CROWD

For a long time, introverts got a bad rap for our love of being alone. But if you think about it, the ability to go solo is something to be thankful for. It frees us up to do what we want and when we want, without worrying about pleasing the group. Of course, we do enjoy the company of others at times. But we are happy to be the lone wolf for a while, knowing that there is wisdom and freedom in solitude. Being an independent introvert also means that you don't get lost in the crowd. Instead, you navigate by your own inner starlight and always know how to find your way home.

November 6

#3 You're Not a Busybody

Busyness has become a trend, and extroverts have latched onto it like it's the last pair of parachute pants at an MC Hammer concert. Admittedly, introverts get sucked in by the busybody mentality, too, but we quickly recognize its futility.

A life of constant busyness wears us out while offering little fulfillment. We would much rather focus our limited energy on things that matter to us: our creative outlets, close friends, pets, projects, and fictional friends. This approach creates a life with more meaning and less of the empty filler that the busybody mentality promotes.

November 7

#4 You Think and Feel Deeply

Thinking and feeling deeply can hurt sometimes. It doesn't always feel good to be a deep diver in a world of shallow swimmers. Sometimes, it seems easier to numb our intense feelings and keep our thoughts superficial.

For a long time, I buried my emotions so well I forgot how to find them. But then I realized that the spark of life is fueled by our deepest thoughts and feelings. Emotions literally make us feel more alive, as do ideas, dreams, and lightbulb moments of inspiration. Remember that living in the depths might be turbulent at times, but it's better than flatlining at the surface.

November 8

REFLECTION QUESTIONS

What is one of your strengths that you wish more people would recognize in you? Is there a way for you to more openly express this gift?

Have you been suppressing your emotions? Take a moment to notice what you are feeling right now, and then say thank you for your emotions, even if they seem weak or "ugly."

_____

_____

_____

_____

_____

November 9

#5 YOU DON'T GET BORED

Introverts are rarely bored when we are alone. Our ideas and fantasies are great company. We find endless amusement in our own thoughts, as well as our favorite quiet pastimes. Whatever our passion—reading, writing, drawing, playing video games, or making model airplanes—we become totally engrossed in it, and the outside world ceases to exist. As extroverts relentlessly search for bigger and brighter forms of entertainment, we happily roam the lush landscapes of our inner world, and lose all sense of time.

November 10

#6 You Can Live with Less

Extravagance is an extrovert's game. Introverts tend to be more interested in the simple things in life: a good book, a pumpkin spice latte, time in nature, or a scenic drive with a close friend. Since we are easily overstimulated, introverts gravitate toward a more minimalistic lifestyle. We like our quiet rituals and routines and enjoy a pared-down existence with fewer friends and personal belongings. This allows more space for our heart and mind to expand, without the risk of being overwhelmed.

November 11

#7 You Have the Capacity for Mastery

There are a lot of extremely talented introverts out there. Of course, there are also many gifted extroverts. The thing about introverts is that we are often more likely to put in the hours of solitary practice needed to become exceptional at our craft.

An introvert's love of being alone, combined with our intense, often obsessive focus, propels us to levels of mastery that others can't sit still long enough to achieve. Think Bill Gates, J. K. Rowling, and Bob Dylan. They are all introverts who were single-minded and obsessive enough about their passions to achieve greatness.

November 12

November Fortune Cookie

Let the fortune cookie decide your fate. Roll the dice, and read the fortune that coincides with the number you land on.

1. Your flower will bloom in its own sweet time.
2. Don't let a dark past cast a shadow over today.
3. Don't just think. Take action.
4. You will need to distance yourself from a sinister character.
5. A lost soul is looking for directions to your heart.
6. Like an honorable cat, you will live many lives!

November 13

#8 You Avoid Drama

Conflict-averse introverts tend to avoid drama. This is, indeed, something to be thankful for because drama is a destructive form of distraction. It poisons workplaces and tears friendships apart. While it can be entertaining to watch other people's train-wreck lives on television, we wouldn't want to be part of the wreckage ourselves. Thankfully, most introverts don't have to worry because we're the opposite of drama queens and kings. We're anti-drama townspeople sitting quietly in our hovel, wondering who these Kardashian people are and how the heck they became so famous.

November 14

#9 You Understand the Joy of Missing Out

While extroverts have a Fear of Missing Out (FOMO), introverts don't feel as much of a need to frantically chase every sunset, social gathering, and shiny new activity. We don't live in fear that we'll miss out because we understand the Joy of Missing Out (JOMO). Not only does our lack of FOMO save us money, time, energy, and headaches, it also allows us to truly appreciate the experiences we do have. We can relax into the moment and be thankful that we are exactly where we want to be.

November 15

#10 You Don't Compete for Popularity

Remember when you were in high school and you lived or died by your social status? The popular kids were at the top of the food chain, or so it seemed. As you've probably noticed, being popular in high school doesn't mean much once you enter the "real world." Introverts knew this all along. We understood that having fewer, more meaningful, friendships is where it's at. We are happy to enjoy the warmth of true companionship without all the drama and posturing that comes with being in the in crowd.

November 16

REFLECTION QUESTIONS

List all the gifts you received in solitude this week and give thanks for them—inspiration, connection to a higher power, ideas, or rejuvenation.

What do you enjoy most about "missing out"?

_____

_____

_____

November 17

#11 YOU ARE A CREATIVE BADASS

"The crowd is the gathering place of the weakest; true creation is a solitary act."
—Charles Bukowski, *Sunlight Here I Am: Interviews and Encounters, 1963–1993*

Solitude breeds creativity. Without the distraction of other people, the mind can wander, make connections, and open itself up to an endless expanse of ideas. Be thankful that you have the capacity to endure and actually enjoy the solitude necessary to make great art. After all, creativity is one of the greatest companions an introvert can ask for. She always gives more than she takes and only asks that you provide her with peace, quiet, and a listening ear.

November 18

#12 You Know How to Listen

Introverts know how to listen, not just to words but also to the messages carried on the wings of silence. This is yet another reason why introverts are so perceptive. While others only listen so that they can speak, you listen to understand. This gives you a wiser, more nuanced perspective of the world. Be thankful that you know how to give others the gift of a listening ear, and appreciate the way the act of listening enriches you as a human being.

November 19

#13 You Choose Your Words Carefully

Introverts are word economists in a world of verbal obesity. We know that bloated sentences actually impede connection. They force the listener to wade through an avalanche of unnecessary words to find meaning. Introverts get to the point. Your ability to say more with less is something to be thankful for. After all, this is the secret to being truly heard.

November 20

Monthly Gratitude Moment

As you can see, there are many reasons to be grateful for your introversion. List the qualities you are most grateful for and explore why.

November 21

#14 You Provide an Oasis of Calm

I used to get annoyed when people would tell me that I was "so calm." I saw this as another way of saying that I was boring or strange. No sixteen-year-old teen wants to be compared to Yoda. Now I see things differently. I understand that calmness is a gift, not only to ourselves but also to the people who find peace in our presence. We are a twilight walk and a weekend getaway. We make people feel like they can breathe. That is something to celebrate.

November 22

#15 Landlords Love You

As someone who has moved dozens of times in my life, I am truly grateful that landlords love introverts. I have yet to see an advertisement for a loud, wild, party-loving tenant, and I don't imagine I ever will. Introverts are also quite popular with the elderly, which can be a curse or a blessing depending on how you feel about being set up with someone's adult grandchild ("Oh, aren't you lovely. You would be perfect for our Daniel!").

November 23

#16 YOU CAN FINALLY BE PROUD

Thanks to the introvert revolution, which peaked within the last five years and has been marked by a surge in articles, books, and resources for introverts, the world is finally starting to understand introversion. No longer banished to the world of hermits, misanthropes, and prudish librarians, we can finally break free from stereotypes and show the world who we really are. It truly is a great time to be an introvert.

November 24

REFLECTION QUESTIONS

What are some ways you can show others that you are proud to be an introvert?

Even though we seem calm, introverts get frazzled and stressed just like anyone else. How can you invite more calm into your life this week?

November 25
#17 You Have Patience

Introverts are experts at waiting. We know how to turn time in the dentist's waiting room and passport lineups into a wonderful treat. Instead of growing restless and counting the minutes, we use the time to daydream or flip through the pages of a magazine or book. Since much of human life is spent waiting, having patience is a real gift. We also tend to have a lot of patience with others. Even if we are secretly annoyed on the inside, we usually remain calm and diplomatic until someone really pushes us over the edge, which is an extremely rare occurrence.

November 26
#18 You Have an Internal Reward System

Research has shown that introverts and extroverts respond differently to external rewards. The reason has to do with dopamine, a neurotransmitter that is present in parts of the brain that regulate motivation and pleasure. Introverts are more sensitive to dopamine. Too much of it makes us feel overstimulated. Extroverts, on the other hand, are less sensitive to dopamine. They need more of the feel-good chemical to get the buzz associated with happiness. That's why they are more likely to seek out external rewards, like money, social status, and sex, while introverts weigh internal cues more strongly. Being driven by internal cues helps introverts to cultivate a life of greater meaning and fulfillment.

November 27

#19 You Appreciate the Little Things

As an introvert, you notice the little pleasures that make life sparkle, like that feeling when . . .

- You take your heels off and sink your feet into plush carpets;
- You slip into soft pajamas at the end of a long day;
- An animal friend sleeps on your lap, its furry belly rising and falling;
- You steep yourself in solitude after being surrounded by people;
- You get goosebumps from an unexpected touch;
- You sip champagne bubbles in celebration of . . . anything;
- You fall asleep when you're not supposed to;
- You catch the first familiar whiff of a season:
- spiced pear at Christmas, fresh cut grass in July, warm rain in spring;
- You reunite with a lover in a dream.

>   . . . all the wonderful little feelings!

November 28

Gratitude Challenge

Write a thank you letter congratulating yourself on all your wonderful qualities. Acknowledge the many ways in which your unique characteristics have helped you get to where you are today. Next, mail the letter to yourself. When it returns to you, open it up, read it, and know that the words are true.

November 29

HOW TO BE GRATEFUL WHEN YOU'RE SAD

When we are struggling and feeling down, we are given to hyperbole. We imagine that *everything* is bleak and it *always* has been. The secret to being grateful during difficult times is to look for proof against the hyperbole. For example, if you think that nothing good has ever come of your introversion, look for past evidence that proves otherwise. You might recall a time when a friend thanked you for sitting with her and truly listening. Or you remember how you were able to complete a major project because of your ability to work for long stretches in solitude. Next, start looking for proof closer to the present moment. You'll be amazed at the blessings you uncover when you take the time to look for them.

November 30

NOVEMBER CELEBRATION

I know that November can be a challenging month. But no matter how much you feel like you're failing or falling behind, there is always something to celebrate. Write down what you are proud or excited about today. Remember that any small step in the right direction is worth celebrating.

December

HOLIDAY SURVIVAL

"Christmas gift suggestions: To your enemy, forgiveness. To an opponent, tolerance. To a friend, your heart. To a customer, service. To all, charity. To every child, a good example. To yourself, respect."

—Oren Arnold

December 1

A Recipe for Introvert Bliss

The holiday season can be a tough time for introverts. No one knows this better than I do. Whenever December rolls around (as it does without fail every year), with all its events, endless to-do lists, and obligations, my little innie heart longs to do so much more than my social batteries permit.

As it is, I'm already doing a lot more peopling than usual. I've been out and about shopping for presents and decorations. I've been entertaining a lot more, too. Even though I love solitude, I also love the way my house lights up with warmth and laughter when good friends come over. Still, there comes a point when all the extroverting takes its toll on me. Just when I think my introversion has been "cured" and I can happily fill my days with constant doing and peopling, my body and mind put the brakes on.

I start to get restless and have trouble focusing. The most peculiar thing is that I begin feeling lonely, even though I am socializing more than ever. Over the years, I've come to realize that these are all the warning signs that I'm headed for holiday-induced introvert burnout. The only solution is sweet solitude.

I know that I'm not the only introvert who feels this way at this time of year. It's tough to want to do and be more than your energy levels allow. The thing to remember is that your introversion is a gift, both to you and those around you. When you honor your introverted needs, you become a sanctuary of peace and calm during a time of year when the chaos can be overwhelming to anyone, including our extroverted loved ones. So, please, don't overextend yourself. Take as many time-outs as you need to get through the craziness of December. To help you survive the holiday madness, I've put together a recipe for introverted bliss. This month's entries will give you all the ingredients to stay sane this December.

December 2

A Measure of Patience

Nothing tests an introvert's patience like the relentless hustle and bustle of the holiday season. The crowds, the lineups, the social pleasantries that become increasingly unpleasant—all of these things drain us. When our energy tanks are low we can't help but get irritable, and then we get mad at ourselves for losing our patience. When you feel like everything is going sideways and you can't find your footing, take a deep breath and give yourself as many second chances as you need.

December 3

A Handful of Meaningful Conversations, Small Talk Removed

Some people talk to communicate emotions, ideas, and dreams. Others talk just because they can. Introverts tend to fall into the former camp. That's why the holidays can be so draining and frustrating for us. We face endless hours of meet and greet and constant talking without substance. Seek out the people with whom you can have meaningful conversations, or just laugh and be silly. Reconnect with the old friend who always made you feel at ease. Call the family member who feels like home. Reach out to the other introvert in the room. Remember, all it takes is one moment of connection to get you out of a small talk rut.

December 4
December Book Nook

Here are some lighthearted books to bring you joy and laughter over the holidays.

1. *Introvert Doodles: An Illustrated Look at Introvert Life in an Extrovert World* by Maureen Marzi Wilson
2. *Quiet Girl in a Noisy World: An Introvert's Story* by Debbie Tung
3. *Text, Don't Call: An Illustrated Guide to the Introverted Life* by INFJoe
4. *Introvert Dreams: A Coloring Book Journey* by Andre Sólo, Jenn Granneman, and Maxeem Konrardy
5. *Adulthood is a Myth: A Sarah's Scribbles Collection* by Sarah Andersen

December 5
2–3 Bubble Baths, *Candles Optional

"There must be quite a few things that a hot bath won't cure, but I don't know many of them."
—Sylvia Plath, *The Bell Jar*

The day has been long and you are covered in its cares and worries. Soak it all away in one of life's most affordable luxuries: a hot bubble bath. Immerse your whole body in the sweet relief of warm water; there's nothing else to do but melt into its soothing embrace. This is what self-love looks like over the holidays.

December 6

1 Extra Thick and Delicious Book

One of the best activities to do during a winter storm is to curl up with a book and get lost in its pages. The world can writhe and rage all it wants outside our doors. As long as we have our cozy corner and the company of a few fictional friends, we are content. No matter how busy you are this month, try to steal some time in the early morning or before bed to dip into a good book. I've found that December is a great time to read a style of book that you wouldn't normally choose. If you're usually into non-fiction, give a book of poetry a try. If you love fiction, try memoir. As you might have noticed, the recommendations in this month's Book Nook are mostly illustrated books with a healthy dose of humor. They will give you the chance to laugh and be merry in the comfort of solitude.

December 7

A Dollop of Love from Close Family and Friends

The best part about the holidays is reuniting with beloved family and friends. But for introverts, the reunion can be bittersweet. As much as we love our family, they often drive us crazy. Perhaps you have extroverted family members who don't understand your introversion. They push you to your limits, expecting you to participate in every activity with enthusiasm. A large part of coping with pressure from extroverted family members is learning to find the balance between honoring both your family and yourself. You can do this by planning your "permissions" ahead of time. Decide what events you will give yourself permission to skip. You can also set a time limit on how long you stay at each gathering. If you give yourself permission to leave at 8 p.m., you won't feel guilty for ducking out early, and your family members will be happy you made an effort.

December 8

Unlimited Animal-Friend Cuddles

Pets soothe our introvert soul because it's so easy to make them happy. Food, affection, fresh air—that's all they really want. People are much more complicated. They expect us to stretch and strain ourselves to the point of exhaustion. They want us to fill our social calendar and be busy all the time, especially during the holidays. Meanwhile, cats don't care if we want to spend all day Saturday in our pajamas. As long as we offer food, and the occasional belly rub, they won't judge. The same goes for dogs, hamsters, and parakeets. Their expectations are blissfully low. This is such a relief during the demanding month of December.

December 9

Reflection Questions

If you had all the time in the world over the holidays, what books would you read? If you're not into books, what movies would you watch? Make a book or movie wish list, and don't be surprised if Santa gifts you with some extra time to make your wishes come true.

What permissions will you give yourself over the holidays? For example, maybe you will give yourself permission to say no to two invitations for every one that you accept, or to block off an afternoon for yourself to recover from your office Christmas party.

December 10

A Dash of Magic and Fantasy

"It's important to remember that we all have magic inside us."
—J. K. Rowling

December is a time of year when magic is always within arm's reach. It is the best time to get out of your routine and revisit the wonder of childhood. Go skating, see *The Nutcracker* ballet, listen to Handel's *Messiah*. If you like getting dressed up, go all out for your work Christmas party or find another excuse to get your holiday glam on. There are plenty of opportunities to sparkle in December. You can also add a touch of magic to your own home with music and shimmering decorations or by diving into the fantasy world of books and movies.

December 11

Two Scoops of Solitude

By now, we all know that introverts need solitude to feel at our best. The challenge is asking for space without seeming rude. Society says that we should want to be around people all the time. Meanwhile, our energy needs demand that we take a time-out. So, how do we honor our needs without offending our loved ones?

The first thing to recognize is that it's not wrong to want and need space from those you love. It doesn't mean that you're a horrible Grinch. When you take time out to refuel as an introvert, you will reemerge more present and patient. The next step is to let your loved ones know ahead of time that you'll be taking breaks. That way they won't be surprised or offended when you disappear.

December 12

A Touch of Laughter

Laughter is much needed medicine for introverts who are constantly in mental overdrive. If you've been taking yourself too seriously lately, I've got just the prescription for you. I've prepared a cocktail of hilarity to help you stop overthinking:

The Giggle Cocktail
- A shot of Ellen
- A splash of Missing Missy (www.27bslash6.com/missy.html)
- A half a Hyperbole (www.hyperboleandahalf.blogspot.ca/)
- An infusion of funny cat videos
- Et voila!

December 13

December Fortune Cookie

Let the fortune cookie decide your fate. Roll the dice, and read the fortune that coincides with the number you land on.

1. You will find answers in unusual places.
2. Flow with the rivers of change.
3. A change of perspective will be good for your health.
4. All will go well with your new project.
5. You will face a crossroad soon.
6. Love is right around the corner.

December 14

A Pinch of Do Not Disturb

A few years ago, I spent the holidays with my mother's husband's family in Mexico. I quickly discovered that the holiday festivities in a traditional Mexican household are never-ending, and everyone is expected to participate. I tried my best, but there came a time when I simply had to go to my room, close the door, and hide from the madness. If I can exercise my right to opt out of the festivities during the holidays in Mexico, I'm quite confident that you can do so wherever you are. The secret is to pretend that you are suffering from food poisoning, and limp up to your room with a look of anguish on your face. Or you could just say that you are tired, and leave. It's up to you!

December 15

A Dollop of No

I know that saying no might feel difficult, especially during the holidays. But remember that sometimes no is simply the omission of yes. It's keeping your mouth shut when you're tempted to volunteer your valuable time and energy for something you don't actually want to do. Saying no helps you to create boundaries—not to keep others out, but to keep yourself in. In-trospective. In-ward focused. In-tuitive. In-spired. In-troverted. So, go ahead and say no without guilt.

December 16

A Spoonful of Bribery

There is nothing wrong with a little self-bribery, especially if it means staying sane amidst the holiday madness. Give yourself something to look forward to when you return home from shopping or socializing. Your reward might be a bubble bath and a glass of wine, or popcorn and a movie—whatever gets you through.

December 17

Reflection Questions

Take a moment to write a forgiveness letter to yourself for being less than perfect. Be sure to infuse it with lots of love and compassion.

What little rewards can you give yourself to look forward to amidst the stressful obligations of the holidays?

_____

_____

_____

_____

_____

_____

_____

_____

December 18

A Sprinkling of Gratitude

The children will grow up, the family will spread and expand, the friends will marry and move away. Even the beauty of nature is transient. Be grateful for every moment of shared laughter and love during this season, knowing that nothing is permanent.

December 19

A Cup of Compassion

As humans, we often confuse a sense of duty with compassion. They are not the same thing. We can give to the beggar out of guilt and obligation, but when we feel true compassion, we give from a place of love, humility, and care. You can cultivate compassion by first giving it to yourself. When you are feeling so very rundown and inadequate over the holidays, drop a few coins in your own cup and give yourself a break.

December 20

A Chunk of Guilt-Free Laziness

As citizens of an increasingly productivity obsessed world, we are hardwired to view laziness as a sin. We feel bad for slowing down and doing nothing. Try to see time-outs during the busy holiday season as your right, rather than an offense that will get you on Santa's naughty list. You are not a machine. It's okay to switch off and be blissfully unproductive for a while.

December 21

MONTHLY GRATITUDE MOMENT

As difficult as December may be for introverts, there is much to be grateful for. Write a list of the people and experiences for which you are most grateful this month. Put your heart into it and make it glow.

December 22

A HANDFUL OF SELFISH GIVING

The holidays are known as a time of gift giving. This can be stressful, especially when we are giving in a way that goes against our nature. We think we have to follow traditions and show our love with grand gestures, impressive parties, and expensive gifts. But we are meant to give what feels good to give and make others happy in a way that makes us feel happy. This might mean letting go of fanfare so you can give the gift of your time and attention. Or perhaps, you will give handmade gifts if crafting brings you joy. Remember that a small and simple gift can be more meaningful than an extravagant one.

December 23

A Measure of Oxygen

The holidays are a time when we must constantly direct our energy outward. For introverts who refuel by turning inward, this can create a serious energy deficit. We also start to feel foggy and unfocused. Try as we might to squeeze out every last drop of energy, there comes a point when we are mentally, physically, and emotionally depleted.

There is a writer's saying attributed to Glennon Doyle Melton: "Writing is the exhale, reading is the inhale." Have you been holding your breath this month? Just as writers need to replenish their creative stores by reading, introverts need to restore ourselves by slowing down and taking in air, art, books, and silence.

December 24

Reflection Questions

What is the most compassionate thing you can do for yourself today?

How can you give to your loved ones without going crazy? Is there a win-win way of giving?

_____

_____

_____

_____

December 25

A Piece of Forgiveness

Can you forgive your family and friends for testing your limits over the holidays? More importantly, can you forgive yourself for having a limit? As Kent M. Keith put it in his book *The Silent Revolution: Dynamic Leadership in the Student Council*, "People are illogical, unreasonable, and self-centered. Love them anyway." The easiest way to forgive someone is to take a step back and try to see the true cause of their frustrating behavior. Usually, it has little to do with you and more to do with their insecurities.

December 26

A Slice of Honesty

Go ahead and say what you have been secretly wanting to say—goodness knows you have waited long enough to find the right words. You can blame the magic of the season for making you believe that you can ask for what you want and receive it like a present on Christmas morning. I know it's scary, but it will feel good to finally get it out in the open. So, open your mouth, unravel the words, and just say it, darling.

December 27

A Bushel of "Yay Me!" Moments

Remember when you were really little and everything you accomplished was cause for celebration? Tying your shoes, choosing your clothes for the day, and making your own breakfast were all achievements that made you declare, "Yay me!"

Have a "yay me!" day today by giving yourself a great big pat on the back for every little thing you accomplish. After you make your bed, do laundry, call a friend, or send an email, cheer a silent "Yay me! I did [insert everyday task]." I hope you can tell that this is not meant to be a serious exercise, so don't worry about feeling silly. This is your chance to set the bar blissfully low and have a day of infinite gold stars.

December 28

Holiday Challenge

With the hectic holiday season coming to a close, your challenge is simple: set aside a day to rest and recharge. Daydream, cuddle with an animal friend, indulge, and enjoy a stretch of guilt-free laziness—you've earned it!

December 29

A Dash of Self-Care

You might already know that self-care is important, but do you know how to prioritize it when you're feeling overwhelmed? When you're stretched so thin you look and feel like tissue paper, it's hard to even think of self-care. And yet, that is when you need it most. Here's a tip: when the mere thought of self-care overwhelms you, ask yourself, what is the one self-care practice you can do that will make the biggest difference today? If you're busy, simply making a point to sit down to eat might be the best thing you can do for yourself. Other times, exercising for thirty minutes will do the trick, or adding frozen greens to your meal so you get your vitamins without much effort. The key is to do the thing that feels easy and accessible.

December 30

A Spoonful of Introspection

The end of December is the perfect time to turn inward and reflect on the past year. Look back at all you've accomplished and learned, and acknowledge how far you've come. Ask yourself . . .

- What was the biggest lesson I learned?
- What am I most proud of?
- What would I do differently?
- What do I want more of in the coming year?

Baking Instructions:
Combine all the ingredients for innie bliss, and knead with self-love until soft and pliable. Place in a giant, Earth-sized snow globe and pray that you make it to the New Year.

December 31

December Celebration

If you look back at all the things you did this month, you'll probably find that there is a lot to celebrate. Just making it through the month of December is something to cheer about. Write down your top celebration in your journal.

Reading List

Andersen, Sarah. *Adulthood is a Myth: A Sarah's Scribbles Collection.* Kansas City: Andrews McMeel Publishing, 2016.

Aron, Elaine. *The Highly Sensitive Person: How to Thrive When the World Overwhelms You.* New York: Harmony Books, 1997.

Blanton, Brad. *Radical Honesty: How to Transform Your Life by Telling the Truth.* Stanley: Sparrowhawk Publications, 2005.

Brown, Brené. *Daring Greatly: How the Courage to Be Vulnerable Transforms the Way We Live, Love, Parent, and Lead.* New York: Avery Publishing, 2015.

Brown, Brené. *The Gifts of Imperfection: Let Go of Who You Think You're Supposed to Be and Embrace Who You Are.* Center City: Hazelden Publishing, 2010.

Brenner, Helene. *I Know I'm in There Somewhere: A Woman's Guide to Finding Her Inner Voice and Living a Life of Authenticity.* New York: Avery Publishing, 2004.

Cagen, Sasha. *Quirkyalone: A Manifesto for Uncompromising Romantics.* San Francisco: HarperOne, 2006.

Cain, Susan. *Quiet: The Power of Introverts in a World That Can't Stop Talking.* New York: Broadway Books, 2012.

Cameron, Julia. *The Artist's Way: 25th Anniversary Edition*. New York: TarcherPerigee, 2002.

Campbell, Joseph. *The Hero's Journey: Joseph Campbell on His Life and Work*. Novato: New World Library, 1990.

Campbell, Joseph. *The Hero With a Thousand Faces*. New Jersey: Princeton University Press, 1973.

Chapman, Gary. *The Five Love Languages: The Secret to Love that Lasts*. Chicago: Northfield Publishing, 2014.

Chbosky, Stephen. *The Perks of Being a Wallflower*. New York: MTV Books, 2010.

Chung, Michaela. *The Irresistible Introvert: Harness the Power of Quiet Charisma in a Loud World*. New York: Skyhorse Publishing, 2016.

Coelho, Paulo. *The Alchemist*. San Francisco: HarperOne, 2005.

Dembling, Sophia. *The Introvert's Way: Living a Quiet Life in a Noisy World*. New York: TarcherPerigee, 2012.

Dembling, Sophia. *Introverts in Love: The Quiet Way to Happily Ever After*. New York: TarcherPerigee, 2015.

Edberg, Pia. *The Cozy Life: Rediscover the Joy of the Simple Things Through the Danish Concept of Hygge*. Charleston: CreateSpace Independent Publishing, 2016.

Egan, Kerry. *On Living*. New York: Riverhead Books, 2016.

Fine, Debra. *The Fine Art of Small Talk: How to Start a Conversation, Keep It Going, Build Networking Skills—and Leave a Positive Impression!*. New York: Hachette Books, 2005.

Fitch, Janet. *White Oleander: A Novel*. New York: Back Bay Books, 2000.

Gaiman, Neil. *The Ocean at the End of the Lane: A Novel*. New York: William Morrow and Company, 2013.

Gilbert, Elizabeth. *Big Magic: Creative Living Beyond Fear*. New York: Riverhead Books, 2015.

Elizabeth Gilbert et al. *Eat Pray Love Made Me Do It: Life Journeys Inspired by the Bestselling Memoir*. New York: Riverhead Books, 2016.

Granneman, Jenn. *The Secret Lives of Introverts: Inside Our Hidden World*. New York: Skyhorse Publishing, 2017.

Granneman, Jenn, Maxeem Konrardy, and Andre Sólo. *Introvert Dreams: A Coloring Book Journey*. Quebec: Northwest Passage Books, 2016.

Greger, Michael. *How Not to Die: Discover the Foods Scientifically Proven to Prevent and Reverse Disease*. New York: Flatiron Books, 2015.

Hay, Louise. *Gratitude: A Way of Life*. Carlsbad: Hay House, 1996.

Hanh, Thich Nhat. *True Love: A Practice for Awakening the Heart*. Boulder: Shambhala, 2004.

Helgoe, Laurie. *Introvert Power: Why Your Inner Life Is Your Hidden Strength*. Naperville: Sourcebooks, 2013.

Heller, Rachel, and Amir Levine. *Attached: The New Science of Adult Attachment and How It Can Help You Find—and Keep—Love*. New York: TarcherPerigee, 2012.

Hoff, Benjamin. *The Tao of Pooh*. London: Penguin Books, 1983.

Howes, Lewis. *The Mask of Masculinity: How Men Can Embrace Vulnerability, Create Strong Relationships, and Live Their Fullest Lives*. Emmaus: Rodale Books, 2017.

INFJoe. *Text, Don't Call: An Illustrated Guide to the Introverted Life*. New York: TarcherPerigee, 2017.

Jay, Francine. *The Joy of Less, A Minimalist Living Guide: How to Declutter, Organize, and Simplify Your Life*. Medford: Anja Press, 2010.

Kalanithi, Paul. *When Breath Becomes Air*. New York: Random House, 2016.

Keith, Kent M. *The Silent Revolution: Dynamic Leadership in the Student Council*. Terrace Press, 2003.

King, Stephen. *On Writing: A Memoir of The Craft*. New York: Scribner, 2000.

Kleon, Austin. *Steal Like an Artist*. New York: Workman Publishing Company, 2012.

Kondo, Marie. *The Life-Changing Magic of Tidying Up: The Japanese Art of Decluttering and Organizing.* Berkeley: Ten Speed Press, 2014.

Kralik, John. *A Simple Act of Gratitude: How Learning to Say Thank You Changed My Life.* New York: Hachette Books, 2011.

Kurtz, Adam. *1 Page at a Time: A Daily Creative Companion.* New York: TarcherPerigee, 2014.

Lamott, Anne. *Bird by Bird: Some Instructions on Writing and Life.* New York: Anchor Books, 1995.

Lesowitz, Nina, and Mary Beth Sammons. *Living Life as a Thank You: The Transformative Power of Daily Gratitude.* Jersey City: Viva Editions, 2009.

Markowitz, David. *Self-Care for the Self-Aware: A Guide for Highly Sensitive People, Empaths, Intuitives, and Healers.* Carlsbad: Balboa Press, 2013.

Niequist, Shauna. *Bittersweet: Thoughts on Change, Grace, and Learning the Hard Way.* New York: Zondervan, 2013.

Northrup, Christiane. *Women's Bodies, Women's Wisdom (Revised Edition): Creating Physical and Emotional Health and Healing.* New York: Bantam Books, 2010.

Olsen Laney, Marti. *The Introvert Advantage: How Quiet People Can Thrive in an Extrovert World.* New York: Workman Publishing Company, 2002.

Orloff, Judith. *Emotional Freedom: Liberate Yourself from Negative Emotions and Transform Your Life.* New York: Harmony Books, 2010.

Orloff, Judith. *The Empath's Survival Guide: Life Strategies for Sensitive People.* Louisville: Sounds True, 2017.

Palmer, Amanda. *The Art of Asking: How I Learned to Stop Worrying and Let People Help.* New York: Grand Central Publishing, 2014.

Ravikant, Kamal. *Love Yourself Like Your Life Depends On It.* Charleston: CreateSpace Independent Publishing, 2012.

Rivera, Diego, with Gladys March. *My Art, My Life: An Autobiography.* New York: Dover Publications, 1992.

Ruiz, Don Miguel. *The Four Agreements: A Practical Guide to Personal Freedom*. San Rafael: Amber-Allen Publishing, 1997.

Schafer, Jack. *The Like Switch: An Ex-FBI Agent's Guide to Influencing, Attracting, and Winning People Over*. New York: Touchstone Books, 2015.

Schultz, Frances, Trevor Tondro, and Newell Turner. *The Bee Cottage Story: How I Made a Muddle of Things and Decorated My Way Back to Happiness*. New York: Skyhorse Publishing, 2015.

Schumer, Amy. *The Girl with the Lower Back Tattoo*. New York: Gallery Books, 2016.

Shoshanna, Brenda. *Zen and the Art of Falling in Love*. New York: Simon & Schuster, 2004.

Silverstein, Shel. *Every Thing on It*. New York: HarperCollins, 2011.

Sincero, Jen. *You Are a Badass: How to Stop Doubting Your Greatness and Start Living an Awesome Life*. Philadelphia: Running Press, 2013.

Smith, Myquillyn. *The Nesting Place: It Doesn't Have to Be Perfect to Be Beautiful*. Grand Rapids: Zondervan, 2014.

Strayed, Cheryl. *Wild: From Lost to Found on the Pacific Crest Trail*. New York: Vintage Books, 2013.

Swan, Teal. *Shadows Before Dawn: Finding the Light of Self-Love Through Your Darkest Times*. Carlsbad: Hay House, 2015.

Tung, Debbie. *Quiet Girl in a Noisy World: An Introvert's Story*. Kansas City: Andrews McMeel Publishing, 2017.

Williamson, Marianne. *A Return to Love: Reflections on the Principles of "A Course in Miracles"*. San Francisco: HarperOne, 1996.

Wilson, Maureen Marzi. *Introvert Doodles: An Illustrated Look at Introvert Life in an Extrovert World*. Avon: Adams Media, 2016.

Acknowledgments

I would like to extend a big thank you to everyone at Skyhorse for making this book possible. I am especially grateful to my editor, Kim Lim, for believing in *The Year of The Introvert* and helping bring it to life.

The members of my introvert community who have supported my work for years also deserve a huge thank you. Without you, none of this would be possible.

Thank you to my mother, Jane Darling, and my grandmother, Sylvia Adams, for always believing in me.

A Note from the Author

Before I was an author, I was a blogger. I would love it if you joined the hundreds of thousands of introverts from around the world who follow my blog, *Introvert Spring*. There are a wealth of free resources on the site, as well as on my various social media platforms.

How to find more of my introvert resources:

Step 1: Visit my website www. introvertspring.com and enter your email address to get two free ebooks and free articles I do not share on the site.

Step 2: Like my Introvert Spring Facebook page so you never miss a thing. I regularly share introvert articles, memes, cartoons, and infographics on the page, which has over 100,000 followers.

Step 3: Navigate to the blog section of my website and dig into the hundreds of free videos, articles, and infographics available. These resources have been created with the specific challenges and strengths of introverts in mind. I'd love to be your guide as you embrace your introversion and live your best innie life.